Interpreting Assessment Data

Interpreting Assessment Data
Statistical Techniques You Can Use

by Edwin P. Christmann
and John L. Badgett

NSTApress
National Science Teachers Association

Arlington, Virginia

Claire Reinburg, Director
Jennifer Horak, Managing Editor
Judy Cusick, Senior Editor
Andrew Cocke, Associate Editor
Betty Smith, Associate Editor

ART AND DESIGN
Will Thomas Jr., Director
Tim French, Cover and Interior Design

PRINTING AND PRODUCTION
Catherine Lorrain, Director
Jack Parker, Electronic Prepress Technician

NATIONAL SCIENCE TEACHERS ASSOCIATION
Francis Q. Eberle, PhD, Executive Director
David Beacom, Publisher

Library of Congress Cataloging-in-Publication Data

Christmann, Edwin P., 1966-
  Interpreting assessment data : statistical techniques you can use / by Edwin P. Christmann and John L. Badgett.
     p. cm.
  Includes index.
  ISBN 978-1-933531-36-6
  1. Educational tests and measurements--Statistics. 2. Students--Rating of--Statistics. 3. Academic achievement--Statistics. 4. Statistical analysis. I. Badgett, John L. II. Title.
   LB3051.C527 2008
   371.26--dc22
                                    2008035942

Contents

ABOUT THIS BOOK

This textbook is designed for use with introductory educational assessment courses, science education courses, and inservice science teacher development. It presents a nonthreatening, practical approach to educational assessments and statistics with the template for applications of the graphing calculator. It is our hope that we have created a resource that gives science teachers and educational planners the means to examine prescribed teaching methodologies for the teaching and assessment of higher-order thinking skills within the school curricula. The book is based on the National Standards for Educational Testing (AERA, APA, NCME 1999) and the National Science Education Standards and coincides with the No Child Left Behind Act.

The book begins with an overview of the development and current purposes of educational assessment and some of the individuals who have played significant roles in this movement that spans more than 2,000 years. Then it introduces statistical analysis in a nonthreatening and statistically friendly manner that presents a variety of ways for teachers to examine and calculate data on students' performances. As a bonus, these chapters furnish clear instructions for making computations by hand and by calculator. You will need only a very basic knowledge of mathematics to master the content in these chapters.

The chapters on statistics demonstrate how to organize test and assessment data. Also, they introduce scales of measurement, the normal curve, and skewed distributions of data. Chapter 3 will familiarize you with the concepts of central tendency (the mean, the median, and the mode) and variation (standard deviation and variance). Knowledge of these basic statistical concepts, which you will apply to classroom test and assessment data, provides a foundation for all other classroom applications of educational measurements and statistics concepts.

An orientation to the procedures that enable you to determine class rank, percentile rank, and standard scores from either classroom or norm-referenced data is followed by an introduction to the concept of correlation that demonstrates the different assessment instruments. Finally, the book scaffolds the statistical applications for an easy understanding of validity and reliability. The final chapters explain the importance of test validity and reliability, and also provide step-by-step instructions for determining these necessary components of performance.

Edwin P. Christmann
John L. Badgett

REFERENCE

American Educational Research Association (AERA), American Psychological Association (APA), and National Council on Measurement in Education (NCME). 1999. *Standards for Educational and Psychological Testing.* Washington, DC: AERA, APA, and NCME.

ABOUT THE AUTHORS

Edwin P. Christmann is a professor and chairman of the secondary education department and graduate coordinator of the mathematics and science teaching program at Slippery Rock University in Slippery Rock, Pennsylvania. He is a contributing editor to the National Science Teacher Association's middle school journal *Science Scope* and other journals. He was editor of the NSTA Press book *Technology-Based Inquiry for Middle School*. He teaches graduate-level courses in science education, statistics, testing and measurement, and educational technology.

John L. Badgett is a professor in the secondary education department at Slippery Rock University in Slippery Rock, Pennsylvania, where he teaches graduate courses in quantitative research, qualitative research, and social foundations of education, as well as an undergraduate course in measurements and evaluation. He has published on the relationship between intelligence scores and personality variables and on the effect of different instructional methodologies on student learning.

CHAPTER 1

HOW ASSESSMENT AND TESTING DEVELOPED

OBJECTIVES

When you complete this chapter, you should be able to
1. demonstrate an understanding of the history of testing,
2. list the important personalities of testing,
3. compare and contrast different types of tests,
4. describe the concept of meritocracy,
5. demonstrate an understanding of standardized tests,
6. demonstrate knowledge of computer applications in standardized and classroom testing,
7. discuss the possible effects of the No Child Left Behind Act of 2001 on 21st century education, and
8. demonstrate an understanding of reliability and validity.

Key Terms

When you complete this chapter, you should be able to understand

achievement test
aptitude test
computer-administered test
criterion-referenced test
electronic grade books
equivalent forms
high-stakes testing
intelligence test
meritocracy

No Child Left Behind Act
   (NCLB) of 2001
norm-referenced test
odd-even method
split-halves method
standardized tests
teacher-generated test
test bias
test-retest method

Every government degenerates when trusted to the rulers of the people alone. The people themselves, therefore, are its only safe depositories. And to render even them safe, their minds must be improved to a certain degree.
—*Thomas Jefferson,* Notes on the State of Virginia

The United States has approximately 55 million students in grades K–12. On average, teachers administer 100 teacher-generated tests per school year, which translates into America's students taking approximately 550 million—that's 550,000,000—teacher-generated tests per year. Taking this extraordinary number into consideration, it should be clear that an understanding of testing is essential for teaching practitioners throughout all grade levels and subject areas. Today, if you are a teacher, you need to understand the methods and procedures of educational measurement, not only to be competent, but also to be able to design tests that consistently measure the intended outcomes of your classroom instruction. That is, your tests must be both reliable and valid.

RELIABILITY AND VALIDITY

If a test is reliable, it consistently yields the same results. For example, if you give your students a test, wait a few days and then give them the same test again, the mean scores of the two testing sessions would be similar if the test is reliable. (See Chapter 2 for a discussion of the *mean*.) This method of determining the reliability of a test is called the *test-retest method*.

For some unavoidable reason, your students may be sitting so close to one another during a test that they would have to make a conscientious effort not to see other students' papers. Under such circumstances, you may wish to use *equivalent forms* of the test. With these two methods, you would either place the same items in a slightly different order, or you would phrase the same items in a slightly different manner. In either case, the mean scores of the forms should be similar, if the test is reliable.

You may wish to determine the internal consistency or reliability of your tests. To make such a determination, you would use the *split-halves method*. This method requires that you do one of two things:

1. Compare student responses on the first half of the test against responses on the second half of the test, or

2. Compare student responses on the *odd-even method* because your tests should be steeply graded, which means that the items should be arranged in ascending order of difficulty. Two is more difficult than one, three is harder than two, and so forth. With this format, the student's confidence grows as he or she provides answers.

Without following the proper procedures for educational testing and measurement, the results of teacher-generated classroom tests could be misleading. This book is designed to help you create, along with the guidance of your professor, teacher-generated tests that will yield useful information about your students' learning. Further, this book will widen your knowledge and understanding of standardized tests.

ANCIENT TESTING

No one knows for certain when or where the first formal test was given. Records indicate, however, that around 2000 BC, the Chinese government administered civil service examinations to Chinese citizens and success on these exams resulted in elevated social status. Today, things are not much different in that most people realize that good grades and high test scores improve the odds of landing a higher-paying job. Keep in mind that, for the most part, education, in the United States, and other highly developed Western countries, was restricted until the 20th century to free males who owned land and had the means to afford the school tuition —white males in the United States.

The ascent of Western civilization spawned, about 500 BC, the Golden Age of Greece, during which a society that included philosophers, scientists, mathematicians, artists, and politicians fueled the world's first democracy. Simultaneously, an educational system emerged in which children were tutored at home (Athenians) or attended a military school (Spartans). Between the ages of 18 and 20, Spartan males had to pass a challenging test of fitness, military ability, and leadership skills. Between the ages of 6 and 14, Athenian children studied under the guidance of a teacher, usually a slave, and received an education that included reading the books of Homer, the famous Greek epic poet, and learning how to play the lyre. For the most part, teachers assigned readings and students recited passages back to their teacher. There is no documented use of testing methodologies similar to what we use in schools today.

The Romans, in about 100 BC to AD 200, adopted the Greek system of education and culture. The Romans, however, heightened the emphasis on academic, athletic, and musical competitions among students. According to Morgan (1998), the competitions among students were used as a method to separate people into groups by subject achievement, with the hierarchical position of the categorized group lasting throughout one's life. In the competition boys were asked questions by a teacher until they gave a wrong answer, and the boy who had no incorrect answers was the winner. Keep in mind that a system such as this could be used to rank order the students from the highest achiever to the lowest achiever. The classroom grades and test scores of students today can be used for rank order as well. And, at this point, paper was not readily available. Therefore, books were rare and could be found only in the libraries of major universities.

Between the Dark Ages, beginning around AD 500, and the Enlightenment, about 1700, the methods of assessing students' achievement were not much different from those of the early academies in ancient Greece. In fact, during the Enlightenment, the world's premier universities—Cambridge, Oxford, Paris, and Bologna—emulated the Greek and Roman systems of education. As early as 1219, students at the University of Bologna took law examinations, which resulted in formal credentials.

During the colonial era in the United States, from about 1680 to 1776, a formal education was exclusive to wealthy citizens, who hired tutors to educate their children at home. Academic preparation of students stressed the Latin and Greek classics, which were the foundation for a university education that stressed the liberal arts. Reading and recitation were the primary methods of assessing academic performance during this period. For those who could not afford an academic education, the guild system—encompassing trades such as blacksmith, watchmaker, shoemaker, weaver, and coopers—illustrates one of the first formal systems of performance-based assessment. It linked successful performance of a trade to an apprenticeship and then to a livelihood.

JEFFERSON'S MERITOCRACY

Toward the end of the Enlightenment in America, Thomas Jefferson's *Notes on the State of Virginia* (1782) declared that

> By... [selecting] the youths of genius from among the classes
> of the poor, we hope to avail the State of those talents which

JEFFERSON'S IDEAS ON EDUCATION

Thomas Jefferson's proposal to educate Virginians in his *Notes on the State of Virginia* (1782) stated in part that his goal was

to diffuse knowledge more generally through the mass of the people. This bill proposes to lay off every county into small districts of five or six miles square, called hundreds, and in each of them to establish a school for teaching reading, writing, and arithmetic. The tutor to be supported by the hundred, and every person in it entitled to send their children three years gratis, and as much longer as they please, paying for it. These schools to be under a visitor, who is annually to chuse the boy, of best genius in the school, of those whose parents are too poor to give them further education, and to send him forward to one of the grammar schools, of which twenty are proposed to be erected in different parts of the country, for teaching Greek, Latin, geography, and the higher branches of numerical arithmetic. Of the boys thus sent in any one year, trial is to be made at the grammar schools one or two years, and the best genius of the whole selected, and continued six years, and the residue dismissed. By this means twenty of the best geniusses will be raked from the rubbish annually, and be instructed, at the public expence, so far as the grammer schools go. At the end of six years instruction, one half are to be discontinued (from among whom the grammar schools will probably be supplied with future masters); and the other half, who are to be chosen for the superiority of their parts and disposition, are to be sent and continued three years in the study of such sciences as they shall chuse, at William and Mary college, the plan of which is proposed to be enlarged, as will be hereafter explained, and extended to all the useful sciences. The ultimate result of the whole scheme of education would be the teaching all the children of the state reading, writing, and common arithmetic: turning out ten annually of superior genius, well taught in Greek, Latin, geography, and the higher branches of arithmetic: turning out ten others annually, of still superior parts, who, to those branches of learning, shall have added such of the sciences as their genius shall have led them to: the furnishing to the wealthier part of the people convenient schools, at which their children may be educated, at their own expence. — The general objects of this law are to provide an education adapted to the years, to the capacity, and the condition of every one, and directed to their freedom and happiness.

Source: *http://etext.lib.virginia.edu/toc/modeng/public/JefBv021.html*

nature has sown as liberally among the poor as the rich, but which perish without use if not sought for and cultivated.

As Nicholas Lemann describes in *The Big Test* (1999), Jefferson envisioned the United States as a burgeoning meritocracy, in which society's leaders would be selected solely on the basis of merit. Jefferson's vision stemmed from the belief that the nation needed public schools so that its citizens could receive a free education. Specifically, Jefferson's notes on Virginia unveil a plan for the education of all citizens in the Commonwealth of Virginia, although at the time Native Americans and slaves were not always considered citizens.

Notice that Jefferson's vision of education relied on the judgments of visitors (teachers) to assess the academic abilities of students. This is an early example of high-stakes assessment in that, after the prescribed three years of free education proposed by Jefferson, a child without the financial means for further education who was not recommended by his teacher would not be able to continue his education at the next progressive level—the grammar school. Nonetheless, this is the first proposal for a mass education system in the United States. At the time, it was considered outrageous.

Lemann (1999) points out that the concept of a meritocratic education system is not original with Jefferson but rather with the ancient Greek philosopher Plato, who recommended in *The Republic* that the ideal society be governed by a class of elite citizens. Plato called this system *aristocracy*, defined by Webster as "government by the best individuals or by a small privileged class." The word *meritocracy* applied to the American education system today implies that individuals are segregated on the basis of various levels of academic achievement, in which many of the highest achievers attain prestigious, high-paying jobs as a result of their academic merits.

THE BIRTH OF INTELLIGENCE TESTING

The Enlightenment period opened the door for a scientific explosion in which scientists such as Charles Darwin explained their ideas of natural selection (1859), Gregor Mendel published his work on heredity (1866), Dmitri Mendeleev published his version of the periodic table (1869), and Henri Bequerel discovered the radiation from uranium (1896), to name a few major discoveries. It is with Charles Darwin's cousin, Sir Francis Galton, however, that we find the first examples of the scientific applications of testing.

Sir Francis Galton

Sir Francis Galton can be described as a geographer, meteorologist, tropical explorer, founder of differential psychology, inventor of fingerprint identification, and a pioneer of statistical correlation and regression. He is notoriously known as a eugenicist, which is possibly why many educators today only whisper his name. Galton was instrumental in popularizing eugenics among scientists and influential statisticians during the Victorian and Edwardian eras (about 1840 to 1915). He introduced the word *eugenics* in his book *Hereditary Genius* (1869). The word *eugenics* is defined by Webster as "a science that deals with the improvement of hereditary qualities in a series of generations of a race or breed by social control of human mating and reproduction." Those involved in the eugenics movement identified human intelligence as a characteristic that could be used to establish differences among people.

Galton inquired about the nature and nurture of human intelligence and published his results in several books, including *Hereditary Genius* and *Inquiries Into Human Faculty and Its Development* (1883). Galton was obsessed with taking measurements. He measured death rates, heights, weights, incomes, and virtually any other human characteristic that was quantifiable during his time. He also attempted to develop a test that measured intelligence. His test failed, however, because he attempted to measure irrelevant factors, such as acuity of sight and hearing, sensitivity to slight pressures on the skin, and the speed of reaction to simple stimuli. His greatest contribution to testing is that he provided several statistical methods that are used in educational testing today.

Although not a mathematician, Galton developed the statistical techniques for computing the normal curve, correlation, and regression. The refinement of his statistical techniques was left to his followers, Karl Pearson and Charles Spearman, who will be discussed later in this book, as will the concepts of the normal curve and correlation.

Alfred Binet

In 1905, Alfred Binet furthered the work of Francis Galton by refining instruments to measure human intelligence. As director of the psychology laboratory at the University of Paris, Binet developed an instrument whose single score could identify children who had difficulties in learning. His intent was to use the test as a diagnostic instrument for identifying academic problem areas for remediation. To determine intellectual deficiencies, Binet's test measured reasoning and resulted in a "mental age" score. On the basis of the recommendation of a colleague, German psychologist William Stern, the test taker's mental age would be divided by his or her chronological age in order to compute what is now known as an intelligence quotient, or an IQ.

Later, the resulting intelligence quotient was norm referenced—compared to other test takers' performances—to a comprehensible scale, by multiplying the IQ ratio by 100. A person with a mental age of six and a chronological age of six would have a ratio of one, and multiplying the ratio of one by 100 results in an IQ score of 100, which is the mean IQ score on most intelligence tests used today.

H. H. Goddard

Around 1913, H. H. Goddard, director of research at the Vineland Training School in New Jersey, used the new Binet test to determine the readiness of students. He translated Binet's test into an English version and promoted a more general application of the test's scale. Unlike Binet, Goddard perceived intelligence as a single, innate entity that remained constant over time. During the early stages of intelligence testing, test takers were classified into several categories: *idiots, imbeciles,* and the term that Goddard created himself, *morons,* which he defined as an adult having the mental development of an 8- to 12-year old. Fortunately, these classifications are no longer in use. It is interesting, however, that with the widespread acceptance of intelligence theory among scholars of the period, the early planning of America's public education system likely harnessed the notion of moving to grade levels on the basis of the mental age–chronological age ratio, heralding a system that was to be based on "normal development." Grade levels were assigned as first, second, third, and so forth.

Lewis Terman

Continuing the work of Goddard, Lewis Terman moved standardized intelligence testing to the forefront of psychology and education. After finishing his PhD at Clark University, Terman, who suffered from tuberculosis, went westward and gained a professorship at Stanford University. While at Stanford, he revised Binet's intelligence test to what became the Stanford-Binet Intelligence Test. One of his major contributions was to rescale the test so that a score of 100 became the mean score for test takers at a specific age level. Terman also established the standard deviation of 15 on the test (a statistical concept to be discussed later in this text). His primary interest, however, was researching gifted children. In 1923, he identified more than 1,000 children who participated in his "genius" study. As of January 2003, more than 200 people in the original group, all octogenarians, were still living and providing information to Terman's study for Stanford University researchers.

Another of Terman's contributions was his development of the group intelligence test, which could be administered in 50 minutes. Terman's group test was used to track students by assigning them to different course sequences according to their respective intellectual abilities. In 1917, when the United States entered World War I, Terman collaborated with R. M. Yerkes, a Harvard psychologist, to design tests to screen about 1.75 million army recruits. This in itself may have been one of the most significant factors in the acceptance of testing in American education. By the 1930s, children with high IQs were being "tracked" into "college prep" curricula on the basis of their high scores on Terman's test. That meant that students with higher IQ scores were being prepared for college educations and higher-paying jobs, while those with lower IQs took courses of study that prepared them for lower-paying and, for the most part, more-labor-intensive jobs. Terman believed that no difference existed between the intellectual abilities of males and females; thus, he insisted that females should be accepted into the male-dominated workforce of the early 20th century. Some might argue that the popularity of Terman's test helped open opportunities for females in the professional workforce.

Edward L. Thorndike

Edward L. Thorndike, known as the world's first educational psychologist, was vital in creating structure in the educational measurement field. His contention that "whatever exists at all exists in some amount," not only helped the field of educational psychology but other social sciences as well, including the field of education. Building on the work of John B. Watson, who pioneered the idea of behaviorism, Thorndike's quantitative approach to explaining human learning and intelligence stemmed from earlier experiments with animals that Thorndike had done as a student at Harvard. These experiments resulted in his formulation of the "law of effect," which states that behaviors that are followed by pleasant consequences are strengthened and are more likely to occur in the future. Thus, the "behaviorist" position that human behavior can be explained entirely in terms of reflexes, stimulus-response associations, and the effects of reinforcers in mental terms was adopted. Most educators today, however, associate behaviorism with B. F. Skinner who, during the 1950s, applied his principles of operant conditioning, which posit that change in behavior (i.e., learning behavior) can be achieved only when appropriate reinforcement and feedback are provided.

CHECK FOR UNDERSTANDING

1.1.   Briefly describe the historical roots of intelligence testing.

1.2.   Explain how meritocracy persists in the American education system of today.

1.3.   How did Lewis Terman use Binet's test in America?

1.4.   Basing your explanation on the "law of effect," explain how a student who earns good grades in school might behave toward school in general.

THE RISE OF ACHIEVEMENT TESTING

Although it is reported that short-answer tests were used in the Boston schools during the mid-19th century, achievement testing, designed to measure what students have learned in school, grew out of intelligence testing. In 1923, Terman, who had published the Stanford-Binet Intelligence Test, designed the Stanford Achievement Test. He designed this test to measure student achievement across several subjects in the second through eighth grades. Most important, however, is that Terman administered the test to 350,000 students, giving his test the largest achievement-test sample to date. Terman's work resulted in his Stanford Achievement Test's becoming the model for all future achievement tests.

In 1929, E. F. Lindquist, a professor at the University of Iowa, started a multiple choice–driven scholarship competition for students throughout Iowa. The competition tested students' knowledge of a variety of subjects and was based on the textbooks that public schools used in Iowa. In 1935, the scholarship competition was named the Iowa Tests of Basic Skills (ITBS). It was similar to the Stanford Achievement Test in that it covered all grade levels and curricula areas. Lindquist's ITBS, however, also gave individual school districts a report that compared them to all other school districts throughout Iowa. In addition, the ITBS gave individual student reports, showing the number of correct answers of test takers for each subject-area category. Therefore, the test could be used to evaluate district and teacher success and simultaneously serve as a diagnostic instrument for student strengths and weaknesses.

As word spread about the growing success of the ITBS, other states began to adopt it as a method of measuring subject-area content mastery. By 1940, the test's popularity reached such a high point that that university of Iowa formed a partnership with Houghton Mifflin to distribute the ITBS nationally, resulting in royalties for the university. After that, the achievement-testing market began to expand beyond the Stanford Achievement Test and the ITBS with the addition of the California Achievement Test (CAT), which was published by McGraw-Hill. Harcourt Brace published the Stanford Achievement Test.

High-Stakes Testing

In 1969, the National Assessment of Educational Progress (NAEP) was administered to fourth-, eighth-, and 12th-grade students in reading, writing, mathematics, science, geography, civics, and the arts. The NAEP scores of individual students and schools are not released; rather the test is designed to measure the comparative achievement of students nationwide with respect to their individual states (e.g., how do Texas's eighth-grade students compare to New York's eighth-grade students in mathematics?). Figure 1.1 shows a progressive comparison of average NAEP scores of some states in eighth-grade mathematics. For a complete listing of the results of all levels and subject areas visit *http://nces.ed.gov/nationsreportcard/mathematics/results2003*.

Clearly, the NAEP has had an impact on educational policy making. The No Child Left Behind act has proposed to link federal funding to students' NAEP results. Moreover in 1994, Californians were alarmed by their students' low reading scores on the NAEP. This resulted in a policy shift in reading from whole-language instruction to phonics instruction.

As a *criterion-referenced test,* the NAEP measures knowledge according to specific criteria, and the results are arranged in three categories: basic, proficient, and advanced. Achievement tests such as the CAT, the ITBS, and the Stanford 9 (SAT-9) are *norm-referenced,* which means that the test taker's performance is compared with the performance of other people in a specified reference population. The results of norm-referenced tests are therefore reported as percentile ranks: A student in the 75th percentile has scored at the level of or higher than 75% of his or her peers.

In 1994, Texas introduced the Texas Assessment of Academic Skills (TAAS), which paved the way for state-level evaluation of individual school districts. Pennsylvania has the Pennsylvania System of School Assessment (PSSA); Virginia has the Standards of Learning assessments (SOLs); and other states have followed in the same direction. These state-level tests are being used not only

Figure 1.1

Average Mathematics Scale Scores, Grade 8 Public Schools: by State, 1990–2003

	Accommodations not permitted							Accommodations permitted		
	1990		1992		1996		2000		2000		2003
Nation (Public)[1]	262	*	267	*	271	*	274		272	*	276
Alabama	253	*,**	252	*,**	257	*	262		264		262
Alaska	—		—		278		—		—		279
Arizona	260	*,**	265	*,**	268		271		269		271
Arkansas	256	*,**	256	*,**	262	*	261	*	257	*,**	266
California	256	*,**	261	*,**	263		262	*	260	*,**	267
Colorado	267	*,**	272	*,**	276	*,**	—		—		283
Connecticut	270	*,**	274	*,**	280	*,**	282		281		284
Delaware	261	*,**	263	*,**	267	*,**	—		—		277
Florida	255	*,**	260	*,**	264	*,**	—		—		271
Georgia	259	*,**	259	*,**	262	*,**	266		265	*,**	270
Hawaii	251	*,**	257	*,**	262	*,**	263		262	*	266
Idaho	271	*,**	275	*,**	—		278		277	*	280
Illinois	261	*,**	—		—		277		275		277
Indiana	267	*,**	270	*,**	276	*,**	283		281		281
Iowa	278	*,**	283		284		—		—		284
Kansas	—		—		—		284		283		284
Kentucky	257	*,**	262	*,**	267	*,**	272		270	*,**	274
Louisiana	246	*,**	250	*,**	252	*,**	259	*,**	259	*,**	266
Maine	—		279	*,**	284		284		281		282
Maryland	261	*,**	265	*,**	270	*,**	276		272	*,**	278
Massachusetts	—		273	*,**	278	*,**	283	*	279	*,**	287
Michigan	264	*,**	267	*,**	277		278		277		276
Minnesota	275	*,**	282	*,**	284	*,**	288		287	*	291
Mississippi	—		246	*,**	250	*,**	254	*,**	254	*,**	261
Missouri	—		271	*,**	273	*,**	274	*,**	271	*,**	279
Montana	280	*,**	—		283		287		285		286
Nebraska	276	*,**	278	*,**	283		281		280		282
Nevada	—		—		—		268		265	*,**	268
New Hampshire	273	*,**	278	*,**	—		—		—		286
New Jersey	270	*,**	272	*,**	—		—		—		281
New Mexico	256	*,**	260	*,**	262		260		259	*,**	263
New York	261	*,**	266	*,**	270	*,**	276		271	*,**	280
North Carolina	250	*,**	258	*,**	268	*,**	280		276	*,**	281
North Dakota	281	*,**	283	*,**	284	*,**	283	*,**	282	*,**	287
Ohio	264	*,**	268	*,**	—		283		281		282
Oklahoma	263	*,**	268	*,**	—		272		270		272
Oregon	271	*,**	—		276	*,**	281		280		281
Pennsylvania	266	*,**	271	*,**	—		—		—		279
Rhode Island	260	*,**	266	*,**	269	*,**	273		269	*	272
South Carolina	—		261	*,**	261	*,**	266	*,**	265	*,**	277

Figure 1.1 (cont.)

Average Mathematics Scale Scores, Grade 8 Public Schools: by State, 1990–2003 (cont.)

	Accommodations not permitted								Accommodations permitted		
	1990		1992		1996		2000		2000		2003
South Dakota	—		—		—		—		—		285
Tennessee	—		259	*,**	263	*,**	263		262	*,**	268
Texas	258	*,**	265	*,**	270	*,**	275		273		277
Utah	—		274	*,**	277	*,**	275	*,**	274	*,**	281
Vermont	—		—		279	*,**	283		281	*,**	286
Virginia	264	*,**	268	*,**	270	*,**	277	*	275	*,**	282
Washington	—		—		276	*,**	—		—		281
West Virginia	256	*,**	259	*,**	265	*,**	271		266	*,**	271
Wisconsin	274	*,**	278	*,**	283		—		—		284
Wyoming	272	*,**	275	*,**	275	*,**	277	*,**	276	*,**	284

— Not available.

* Significantly different from 2003 when only one jurisdiction or the nation is being examined.

** Significantly different from 2003 when using a multiple-comparison procedure based on all jurisdictions that participated both years.

[1] National results that are presented for assessments prior to 2003 are based on the national sample, not on aggregated state assessment samples.

Note: Comparative performance results may be affected by changes in exclusion rates for students with disabilities and limited-English-proficient students in the NAEP samples. In addition to allowing for accommodations, the accommodations-permitted results for national public schools (2000 and 2003) differ slightly from previous years' results and from previously reported results for 2000, due to changes in sample weighting procedures.

Significance tests were performed using unrounded numbers. NAEP sample sizes have increased in 2003 compared with previous years, resulting in smaller detectable differences than in previous assessments.

Source: U.S. Department of Education, Institute of Education Sciences, National Center for Education Statistics, National Assessment of Educational Progress (NAEP), 1990, 1992, 1996, 2000, and 2003 Mathematics Assessments.

to evaluate students but also to evaluate teachers, administrators, and school boards. The tests also have an impact on the public and on local economies. After test results are published in local and regional newspapers, they are used to evaluate the quality of school districts. In fact, the operation of some school districts has been taken over by state officials because of low test scores. Moreover, real estate agents are using standardized test scores to market the sale of properties and to determine property value. In addition, issues in education, such as merit pay and school vouchers, are tied to the results of test scores. Standardized testing in America is for high stakes when one considers the kaleidoscope of issues that surround the interpretation of the test scores.

Aptitude Testing

The main difference between an achievement test and an aptitude test is that an *aptitude test* focuses on informal learning and experience, whereas an *achievement test* focuses on the measurement of structured learning objectives. An example of an elementary school–level aptitude test is the Metropolitan Readiness Tests (MRT). The MRT, which takes about 90 minutes to administer, assesses the language and mathematical skills required for early school learning. The test is designed to determine whether a child can make the transition from first grade to second grade and is used by counselors and school psychologists to make class placement decisions.

At the secondary level, a commonly used aptitude test is the SAT Reasoning Test (formerly the SAT-I), which is designed to predict how well a student will do in college. Published by the College Board, the SAT is a nearly four-hour test that measures critical reading (formerly verbal) and mathematical reasoning skills, as well as writing skills. Used in combination with other factors, including class rank, grades, and recommendations, the SAT helps determine a student's readiness to do college-level work. Each of the three sections is scored on a scale of 200 to 800. The test is typically taken by high school juniors and seniors.

The SAT's Evolution

A by-product of the Army Alpha test—the first large-scale IQ test—the SAT was born in the 1920s. Carl Brigham, an assistant to Robert Yerkes, who developed the Army Alpha, adapted the Army Alpha for use as a college admissions tool. It was not until 1933, however, when James Bryant Conant, president of Harvard University, made the decision to offer scholarships to academically talented students from public schools. At the time, students came to Harvard from the most elite boarding schools in the country. The problem for Conant was to find an instrument that would help select the best and brightest students. In this pursuit, he had an assistant dean from Harvard, Henry Chauncey, search for an instrument to help decide on the most qualified candidates for admission to Harvard on scholarship.

After meeting Brigham, Chauncey was convinced that Brigham's SAT met the requirements of a good test on which to base scholarship awards in that it did not strictly rely on the quality of a test taker's prior education. Rather, it was based on intelligence. That meant an academically talented public school student could be identified and selected for admission to Harvard on merit rather than on the basis of having had the privilege of an elite boarding school education.

In 1938 the SAT was used by the members of the College Board to award scholarships. It had replaced all other exams used by the College Board by 1942. During World War II, Chauncey administered the Army-Navy College Qualification Test, a version of the SAT, to more than 300,000 high school seniors, giving him a norm-referenced group (a group of students whose scores served as the basis for assessing subsequent test takers).

On June 22, 1944, President Roosevelt signed the GI Bill, which included funding for World War II veterans to get college educations. Now, with the GI Bill, a college education was within the reach of any veteran who was qualified for admission into a college or university. As a result of the bill, college enrollments soared, creating a drastic need for an instrument to help in the selection of the most qualified applicants.

On December 19, 1947, Henry Chauncey founded the Educational Testing Service (ETS) as the nation's educational testing and research organization. Afterward, the SAT became the standard test for college admissions throughout the United States. American institutions of higher education now had an instrument to facilitate the admissions process. The American College Testing Program (ACT) emerged as the SAT's competition in the 1950s and is used by many colleges and universities today.

It is ironic that the SAT, which was designed to offer underprivileged students scholarships at Harvard, now has become the gatekeeper for the most selective colleges and universities throughout America. In the eyes of the public, the use of the SAT by many colleges and universities has shifted from the flower of a selection instrument to the thorn of a rejection instrument.

CHECK FOR UNDERSTANDING

1.5. How do achievement tests differ from aptitude tests?

1.6. Based on the data presented in Figure 1.1, with accommodations not permitted, identify the 10 states with the highest average mathematics scale scores on the eighth-grade NAEP test and rank them in order from the highest to the lowest score for the year 2000. Is there a geographic pattern within states that you have listed? If so, please explain your answer.

1.7. Using outside references, list five criterion-referenced tests and five norm-referenced tests that are currently used in America's schools.

1.8. The SAT is a byproduct of which test?

1.9. Write a brief biographic statement on the founder of the Educational Testing Service (ETS).

HENRY CHAUNCEY

Henry Chauncey was born in Brooklyn, New York, in 1905. He was the first child of Episcopalian minister Egisto Fabbri Chauncey and attended the Groton School in Groton, Massachusetts. For the Chaunceys, going to Groton was a family tradition, preceding an education at Harvard, for cultivating the necessary manners required of a gentleman. Because of his father's meager salary as the rector of a church in Columbus, Ohio, Chauncey was not able to attend Harvard. So he enrolled at The Ohio State University, a tuition-free public university located in Columbus, Ohio, where he was exposed to psychology professor Herbert Toops. Chauncey was intrigued with Toops, who had studied under E. L. Thorndike, the well-known pioneer of educational testing.

After Chauncey's freshman year at Ohio State, however, his father gathered enough money to transfer him to Harvard. Following his transfer to Harvard, Chauncey looked back on his time at Ohio State as very instructive in that he was introduced to the subject of psychology, which was not then offered at Harvard. During Chauncey's year at Ohio State, Toops had tested the students with aptitude tests designed to predict future college achievement.

Chauncey found this experience especially useful when Carl Brigham asked him to find a test to determine the most qualified students for Harvard scholarships. Moreover, attending Ohio State made Chauncey recognize that many of the students there exhibited as much, if not more, intellectual ability than his peers at Harvard. That was a factor in motivating Chauncey to create an instrument that would help select the best and brightest students for college admission, regardless of their social status. Chauncey, like Jefferson, believed in a meritocracy, where the best and brightest hold positions of importance in society.

CONSTRUCTION OF STANDARDIZED TESTS

As a teacher, you will probably be involved in at least one conversation about the assemblage of standardized tests. For the most part, standardized aptitude and achievement test questions follow similar formats in their construction.

For the SAT, for example, a typical test question spends two years in development. Test items undergo a high level of scrutiny. Members of the math department, examine the math-related items as assurance that each contains a single correct answer and that the procedures for solving each are provided in most high school mathematics curricula. Then, another group of ETS staff members examines the items to make sure they are gender equitable, have no negative connotations for any racial or ethnic group, and are devoid of any referrals to sensitive issues such as violence, terminal diseases, and tragedies.

If they have passed all of the criteria, the items are included in an actual SAT exam, within a selection of questions that will not be factored into the examinees' scores. Then the staff members compute the items' levels of difficulty based on the percentage of students answering each correctly. Each item is placed into a pool of items among those with similar levels of difficulty (*Time* 2003).

As you can see, standardized test development is extremely thorough and objective. Highly trained specialists, whether they are working on the ITBS or the SAT, go through multiple layers of design and pretesting before a test item reaches a test taker. Nonetheless, many people skeptical of standardized testing have accused standardized tests of being biased, which is the topic of our next discussion.

Test Bias

Aptitude and achievement tests are an all-encompassing part of American education. Aptitude tests are used for student placement, while achievement tests are used to measure individual students' progress and to evaluate the effectiveness of academic programs. Standardized testing skeptics debate what content should be covered by these tests and claim that the tests discriminate against different groups of people. Consider, for example, a 1998 SAT test question that was printed in the October 10, 2003, issue of *The Chronicle of Higher Education* (see Figure 1.2). The question was correctly answered by 62% of white test takers but

Figure 1.2

Example of an SAT Question Accused of Being Biased

The dance company rejects _____, preferring to present only _____ dances in a manner that underscores their traditional appeal.

invention ... emergent
fidelity ... long-maligned
ceremony ... ritualistic
innovation...time-honored (correct answer)
custom ... ancient

Source: *The Chronicle of Higher Education* (Oct. 10, 2003)

by only 38% of black test takers, raising a debate as to whether this question is biased.

The test question produced higher scores for one group than another, which is the first issue of test bias. The major case for bias relates to whether the question's content is based on conditions that are more like those experienced by one group than another. If blacks have had limited exposure to the content required for answering this question, the questions may be declared biased against black test takers.

Keep in mind, however, that test companies have committees that represent different ethnicities, social classes, religions, and genders. All standardized questions are carefully screened at various stages before publication with a view to eliminating biased questions. Statistically, assuming that we are comparing norm groups of the same size, it would be nearly impossible to create a test question that has a perfect proportion of correct answers among and between groups that could include males, females, Hispanics, Episcopalians, Native Americans, and more. To combat potential bias, test publishers select samples of minority groups and social classes in proportion to the nation's population and pretest standardized questions accordingly. It is the test publisher's responsibility to report the technical quality of a test and to reduce bias in test construction. Test publishers also should report reliability, validity, and standard error of measurement, which will be discussed in detail later in this book.

National Assessment of Educational Progress

The No Child Left Behind Act of 2001 has had a major impact on local school policies and federal funding throughout America's schools (see Figure 1.3). To receive federal funds, school districts throughout the United States must agree to administer the National Assessment of Educational Progress (NAEP) tests in mathematics and reading to fourth-grade and eighth-grade students. Once the federal government selects the school to be tested, the school must inform parents of the school's participation in the NAEP testing program, although parents are given the opportunity to excuse their children from taking the test and students are not required to answer every question. The school also is required to notify parents and members of the general public that the test can be reviewed by them in a secure location before its administration.

Figure 1.3

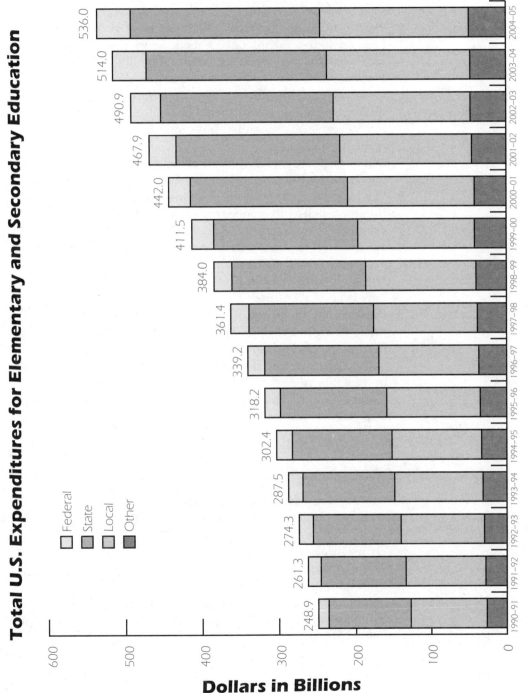

Federal Spending on Public Education in America

Total U.S. Expenditures for Elementary and Secondary Education

Dollars in Billions

Federal
State
Local
Other

600
500
400
300
200
100
0

248.9 1990–91
261.3 1991–92
274.3 1992–93
287.5 1993–94
302.4 1994–95
318.2 1995–96
339.2 1996–97
361.4 1997–98
384.0 1998–99
411.5 1999–00
442.0 2000–01
467.9 2001–02
490.9 2002–03
514.0 2003–04
536.0 2004–05

Years

This graph shows that federal funding for Title I, which provides grants to help disadvantaged children, rose from less than $3 billion in 1980 to more than $7 billion in 2000 and to nearly $14 billion in 2005.

Sources: National Center for Education Statistics, "Common Core of Data" surveys and unpublished statistics. At *www.ed.gov/about/overview/fed/10facts/edlite-chart.html* 2.

District Report Cards

Under the No Child Left Behind Act of 2001, district report cards must contain the following information:

- "Aggregate data on student achievement at each proficiency level on state academic assessments, as well as disaggregated data reflecting race, ethnicity, gender, disability, migrant status, English proficiency, and status as economically disadvantaged;
- Comparison of the above student groups regarding achievement levels on state assessments;
- Percentage of students not tested, disaggregated by student groups;
- Most recent two-year data in achievement by subject area and grade level in areas where assessments are required;
- Aggregated data on state indicators to determine adequate yearly progress, such as attendance rates for elementary schools;
- Graduation rates for secondary schools;
- Information on the district's performance regarding yearly progress, as well as the number, percentage and names of schools identified for improvement, including how long they have been so identified;
- Professional qualifications of teachers, and the percentage of teachers with emergency or provisional credentials;
- Percentage of classes not taught by highly qualified teachers, in the aggregate and disaggregated by schools in the top and bottom quartiles of poverty;
- Comparison of district's students' achievement on state assessments with students in the entire state" (Fissel and Eckerd 2003).

School Report Cards

According to the No Child Left Behind Act of 2001, school report cards must contain the following information:

- "Same information contained on district report card;
- Whether the school has been identified for improvement;
- Information that compares the school's students' achievement on state assessments and indicators of adequate yearly progress with students in the district and the entire state" (Fissel and Eckerd 2003).

Teacher-Generated Tests

Classroom teachers dedicate a great deal of time to the design and administration of tests. One expectation of you as a professional educator is that you will create tests that accurately measure students' learning. Moreover, you should understand that your test results can be used to evaluate the effectiveness of your instruction. The following chapters will show you how to write test questions based on instructional objectives, in a variety of formats, and within the six levels of Bloom's Taxonomy (1956). In addition, this text will take you step-by-step through those statistical procedures that will allow you to determine whether your tests are accurately and consistently measuring what you intend for them to measure in the content areas for elementary and secondary schools and in individual education plans' (IEPs) content, life skills, and prevocational training areas.

Performance-Based Assessment and Portfolios

Although paper-and-pencil tests are suitable for many types of measurement, they are not across-the-board instruments of assessment. For example, a student may be able to write a description of the materials and procedures involved in a lab experiment and correctly answer 48 of 50 multiple-choice items on the creation of websites, but to determine this student's ability to perform the experiment or actually create a website necessitates performance-based assessment. Hence, as you will learn in later chapters, performance-based assessments are essential to any balanced assessment program.

Portfolios can serve as biographies for your students' academic efforts and accomplishments, and they can provide documented evidence of your students' growth and capabilities. If portfolios are to serve as biographies, they must be representative of your students' work, because, if they contain a disproportionate number of unusually good or unusually bad examples of a student's work, they serve only to distort and misrepresent. Also, a student's portfolio should contain proportionate and representative samples of his or her performance within the different levels of Bloom's Taxonomy, which will be discussed throughout the text.

As with tests, any student performance or portfolio should be part of your instructional objectives. These objectives should serve as blueprints for all of your instructional efforts. Through the following chapters, you will learn how to write clear and measurable objectives that will prescribe precisely what you may expect from your students and, in turn, will make your assessments more accurate and meaningful. In addition, you will be able to construct instructional objectives that will serve as the basis for a variety of test items, performance-based assessments, and possible portfolio inclusions within the major content areas of the elementary and secondary schools and the IEP content, life skills, and prevocational training areas.

Computerized Testing

The use of computerized testing in everyday life, such as for obtaining a driver's license, shows that technology is prevalent within the field of testing and measurement. Moreover, using computers to take standardized tests, such as the Praxis and Graduate Record Examination (GRE), is also becoming widespread in the field of education. With a *computer-administered test,* questions appear on the computer monitor, and the test taker gives responses with the keyboard or mouse. The benefits of using the computer are that it saves time and money and gives rapid feedback to the test taker.

Several different computerized technologies are available for classroom testing and measurement applications. One of the greatest innovations for teachers is the electronic grade-book programs that generate seating charts and organize class records such as grades, absences, and discipline problems (see Chapter 8, p. 172). In addition, grade-book software packages calculate grades and generate reports.

CHECK FOR UNDERSTANDING

1.10. List some steps that can be involved in the creation of an SAT test question.

1.11. How could test bias occur on a teacher-generated test? Please explain your answer.

1.12. What would be the major impact on a school district if it failed to comply with the requirements of the No Child Left Behind Act of 2001?

1.13. Use the internet and the search engine of your choice to search for at least five grade-book software packages. If possible, download trial versions of two or three software packages for evaluation. Based on your evaluations, which software package would you select for your classroom? Please explain your answer.

IN SUMMARY

Teachers make multiple decisions each day regarding their students, and an overwhelming majority of these decisions are immune to quantification. When responding to such situations, you must attempt to be objective within a qualitative framework. Fortunately, there are assessment decisions that you can make from a quantitative baseline, but only if you are aware of the potential applicability of quantitative assessment to the situation in question. Once instituted, this type of assessment offers fairer evaluations of students and professional justification for the teacher.

Most educators and laypersons will agree that high-stakes decisions are more readily accepted if they are based on quantitative criteria, such as scores on standardized tests. Grades, however, although usually factored into the equations for high-stakes decisions, are sometimes based on nebulous and unexplainable perceptions, which may either raise questions about fairness to the student or invite accusations of grade inflation. Hence, it is important that teachers assess their students' performance in accordance with predetermined objectives and consistent criteria. This book will give you the information you need to construct such criteria with respect to both the formative (ongoing) and summative (conclusive) assessment that follow sequential teaching.

CHAPTER REVIEW QUESTIONS

1.14. Compare and contrast Thomas Jefferson and Henry Chauncey by listing three similarities and three differences between them.

1.15. List two differences between an individual intelligence test and a group intelligence test. Who developed the first group intelligence test and what was its first application?

1.16. Explain how the NAEP differs from a typical achievement test such as the ITBS.

1.17. Which type of test focuses on informal learning and experience? Please give an example of this type of test.

1.18. Why did Carl Brigham adopt the SAT for use at Harvard University?

1.19. Give an example of test bias, and explain how this type of test bias can be minimized or removed.

1.20. How would a low graduation rate reported in a District Report Card affect a school district's status with respect to the No Child Left Behind Act of 2001? What are some of the possible consequences?

Interpreting Assessment Data

1.21. List three advantages of a computer-administered test over a traditional paper-and-pencil test.

1.22. List at least five applications of electronic grade-book software packages and three ways that these applications improve classroom instruction.

ANSWERS: CHECK FOR UNDERSTANDING

1.1. This answer will vary; please see instructor.

1.2. This answer will vary; please see instructor.

1.3. Terman adapted Binet's test at Stanford University so that he could measure genius-level IQ scores.

1.4. Based on the "law of effect" a student who does well in school would behave positively toward school.

1.5. Achievement tests measure recent learning whereas aptitude tests are designed to measure innate abilities.

1.6. Minnesota, Montana, Maine, Kansas, Massachusetts, North Dakota, Ohio, Vermont, Connecticut, and Nebraska. Four of the 10 top achievers are from the Northeastern region of the United States.

1.7. This answer will vary; please see instructor.

1.8. Carl C. Brigham's Army IQ tests.

1.9. This answer will vary, please see instructor.

1.10. Writing it,
reviewing it,
trying it out,
placing it on the test,
vetting the test,
making final changes, and
the final version

1.11. Test bias can occur when the question's content is based on conditions that are more like those experienced by one group than another. Classroom teachers need to be sensitive to a variety of factors, such as culture, gender, race, and religion.

1.12. The school district could face punitive measures.

1.13. The answers will vary; please see instructor.

ANSWERS: CHAPTER REVIEW QUESTIONS

1.14. The answer will vary; please see instructor.

1.15. Individual IQ tests are more time consuming and more expensive to administer than group IQ tests. Lewis Terman is credited with the design of the first group IQ test.

1.16. The NAEP scores of individual students and schools are not released; rather the test is designed to measure the achievement of students nationwide with respect to their states. The ITBS, however, is purchased by individual school districts and is used to measure the achievement of students within different classrooms at a variety of grade levels.

1.17. An aptitude test focuses on informal learning and experience, whereas an achievement test focuses on the measurement of structured learning objectives.

1.18. He wanted to give scholarships based on merit.

1.19. The major case for bias relates to whether the question's content is based on conditions that are more like those experienced by one group than another. The best way to minimize bias is to remove questions that have the potential for bias.

1.20. A low graduation rate could result in action against the school district.

1.21. It saves time and money, and gives rapid feedback to the test taker.

1.22. Electronic grade books let you enter student names, generate seating charts, and organize class records such as grades, absences, and discipline problems. In addition, grade-book software packages calculate grades and generate reports.

LINKS TO TESTING WEBSITES

ACT: Information for Life's Transitions
  www.act.org
American Educational Research Association
  www.aera.net
Buros Institute of Mental Measurements
  www.unl.edu/buros/bimm/index.html
The College Board
  www.collegeboard.com
CTB McGraw-Hill
  www.ctb.com
Educational Testing Service
  www.ets.org
ERIC Clearinghouse on Assessment and Evaluation
  www.ericae.net

National Center for Research on Evaluation, Standards, and Student Testing (CRESST)
www.cse.ucla.edu
National Council on Measurement in Education (NCME)
www.ncme.org
Psychological Assessment Resources, Inc. (PAR)
www.parinc.com
Riverside Publishing
www.riverpub.com
Sylvan Learning Systems, Inc.
www.educate.com

REFERENCES

Binet, A., and T. Simon. 1916. *The development of intelligence in children.* Baltimore: Williams and Wilkins. (Reprinted 1973, New York: Arno Press; 1983, Salem, NH: Ayer.)

Bloom, B. S. 1956. *Taxonomy of educational objectives, Handbook 1: Cognitive domain.* New York: David McKay.

Fissel, E. F., and C. L. Eckerd. August, 2003. NCLB Update: District and School Report Cards. *PSBA Bulletin 20–22.*

Galton, F. 1869. *Hereditary genius: An inquiry into its laws and consequences.* London: Macmillan.

—1883. *Inquiries into human faculty and its development.* New York: Dutton.

Jefferson, T. 1782. *Notes on the State of Virginia.* Paris: privately printed. Also at *http://etext.lib.virginia.edu/toc/modeng/public/JefBv021.html.*

Lemann, N. 1999. *The big test: The secret history of the American meritocracy.* New York: Farrar, Straus and Giroux.

Morgan, W. G. 1998. Test developer profile: Christiana D. Morgan. In R. J. Cohen and M. E. Swerdlik, *Psychological testing and assessment: An introduction to tests and measurements, 4th ed.* Mountain View, CA: Mayfield.

Time. 2003. at *www.time.com/time/covers/1101031027/sosat_question.html.* Posted Sunday, October 19.

FURTHER READING

Bergin, D. A., and G. J. Cizek. 2001. *Alfred Binet.* In X *Fifty major thinkers on education: From Confucius to Dewey,* ed. J. A. Palmer, 160–164. London: Routledge.

Binet, A. 1916. New methods for the diagnosis of the intellectual level of subnormals. In *The development of intelligence in children,* E. S. Kite (trans.). Vineland, NJ: Publications of the Training

School at Vineland. (Originally published 1905 in *L'Année Psychologique 12*, 191–244.)

Clariana, R., and P. Wallace. 2002. Paper-based versus computer-based assessment: Key factors associated with the mode effect. *British Journal of Educational Technology* 33 (5): 593-602.

Dubois, P. H. 1970. *A history of psychological testing.* Boston: Allyn and Bacon.

Fancher, R. E. 1985. *The intelligence men: Makers of the IQ controversy.* New York: W. W. Norton.

Goddard, H. H. 1920. *Human efficiency and levels of intelligence.* Princeton, NJ: Princeton University Press.

Hirsch, E. D. 1996. *The schools we need: Why we don't have them.* New York: Doubleday.

Hothershall, D. 2004. *History of psychology.* New York: McGraw Hill.

Murchison, C. 1930. *History of psychology in autobiography: Autobiography of Lewis Terman* Vol. 2, 297–331. Worcester, MA: Clarke University Press.

Shepard, L. A. 2000. The role of assessment in learning culture. *Educational Researcher* 29 (7): 4–14.

Siegler, R. S. 1992. The other Alfred Binet. *Developmental Psychology* 28: 179–190.

Wolf, T. H. 1973. *Alfred Binet.* Chicago: University of Chicago Press.

Young, J. R. October 2003. Researchers charge racial bias on SAT. *Chronicle of Higher Education* 50 (7): A34-A35

APPENDIX TO CHAPTER 1

Historical Timeline of Educational Testing	
2000 BC	Chinese civil service testing is administered.
500 BC	Spartan males are tested in military skills.
387 BC	Plato suggests that the brain is a mechanism for mental processes.
335 BC	Aristotle proposes that the heart is the mechanism of mental processes.
AD 1219	Law examinations are administered at Medieval University of Bologna.
AD 1859	Charles Darwin publishes *On the Origin of Species*.
AD 1869	Sir Francis Galton, influenced by his cousin Charles Darwin's publication of the *Origin of Species*, publishes *Hereditary Genius*. Galton argues that intellectual abilities are genetic in nature.
AD 1878	G. Stanley Hall earns the first American PhD in psychology. He later was the founder of the American Psychological Association (APA).
AD 1888	James Cattell develops a series of psychological and cognitive tests at the University of Pennsylvania.
AD 1890	William James publishes *Principles of Psychology*.
AD 1891	James Cattell founds the Psychological Laboratory at Columbia University.
AD 1895	Alfred Binet founds the first laboratory school at the University of Paris.
AD 1897	Joseph Rice measures spelling achievement.
AD 1898	Edward Thorndike develops the "law of effect."
AD 1904	Charles Spearman introduces the two-factor theory of intelligence. E. L. Thorndike publishes *Introduction to the Theory of Mental and Social Measurements*.
AD 1905	Alfred Binet publishes his first intelligence test, known as the Binet-Simon test. Lewis Terman completes his dissertation on "Genius and Stupidity: A Study of Some of the Intellectual Processes of Seven 'Bright' and Seven 'Stupid' Boys" at Clark University. Henry Chauncey is born.
AD 1907	Charles Spearman introduces the term *reliability coefficient*.
AD 1911	Edward Thorndike publishes his first article on animal intelligence, leading to the theory of operant conditioning.
AD 1912	William Stern develops the original formula for the intelligence quotient (IQ) after studying the scores on Binet's intelligence test.
AD 1913	John E. Watson publishes *Psychology as a Behaviorist Views It*.
AD 1916	Lewis Terman publishes the Stanford-Binet Intelligence Test.
AD 1917	Robert Yerkes (president of APA at the time) develops the Army Alpha and Beta Tests to measure intelligence in a group format. The tests were adopted for use with all new recruits in the U.S. military a year later.
AD 1918	Otis Group intelligence scale is published.

AD 1923	C. C. Brigham publishes *A Study of American Intelligence*.
AD 1929	E. F. Linquist, University of Iowa professor, designs an achievement test to be used at the Iowa Academic Meet. This was the early version of the Iowa Tests of Basic Skills.
AD 1932	Jean Piaget publishes *The Moral Judgment of the Child*.
AD 1933	C. C. Brigham creates the SAT Test.
AD 1937	Kuder and Richardson publish K-R 20 reliability coefficient in *Psychometrika*.
AD 1939	Wechsler-Bellevue Intelligence Test is published; it eventually became a widely used intellectual assessment.
AD 1942	Jean Piaget publishes *Psychology of Intelligence*, which introduces human cognition and development.
AD 1947	Educational Testing Service is founded.
AD 1953	B. F. Skinner publishes *Science and Human Behavior*.
AD 1957	Russians launch Sputnik.
AD 1965	The Elementary and Secondary Education Act (ESEA), commonly known as Title I, is passed.
AD 1983	*A Nation at Risk* is published by the Carnegie task force. The report shows that American students' achievement scores are in a state of decline.
AD 1993	Goals 2000 is established and sets standards for American students to be "the best."
AD 2001	The No Child Left Behind Act is passed.

Chapter 2

SCALES AND NUMBER DISTRIBUTIONS

OBJECTIVES

When you complete this chapter, you should be able to
1. demonstrate an understanding of the different scales of measurement and how they relate to educational measurement;
2. compare and contrast the different types of data as they relate to educational measurement;
3. select, create, and use appropriate graphical representations of data, including histograms;
4. represent data using tables and graphs such as line plots, bar graphs, and line graphs;
5. recognize and generate equivalent forms of decimals through rounding; and
6. describe the shape and important features of a set of data and compare related data sets, with an emphasis on how the data are distributed in school settings.

Key Terms

When you complete this chapter, you should be able to understand

array	histogram
bar graph	interval scale
bell curve	nominal scale
Cartesian grid	normal curve
continuous variable	normal distribution
discrete variable	ordinal scale
distribution	ratio scale
frequency distribution	rounding numbers
frequency graph	simple bar graph
frequency polygon	skewed distributions
frequency table	variables

Statistics is a branch of science that deals with the collection, analysis, interpretation, and presentation of numerical data. We use statistics every day to solve problems. Geneticist Gregor Mendel, for example, experimented with pea plants, which led to the development of theories of dominant and recessive genes. Similarly, teachers use statistics to average classroom grades to determine what students have learned as a result of classroom instruction. In this chapter, we will demonstrate how you can use the powerful tool of descriptive statistics in your classroom to help you summarize, organize, and simplify data.

To use statistics, we must first take measurements. According to Allen and Yen (2002), measurement is "the assigning of numbers to individuals in a systematic way as a means of representing properties of the individuals." For example, when you look at a thermometer and note that the outside temperature is 67°F, you have measured the temperature, but what does this measurement mean? In itself, it's just a number. When we arrange measurements into scales, however, we can begin to understand and to compare them. This is what teachers do with statistics when taking measurements of student performance, both formative—ongoing measurements—and summative—end-of-the-semester measurements. That is, they measure student performance on a continual—formative—and on a final basis—summative.

As you already may have found, test scores are sometimes not easy to interpret. For example, if a student scored a 610 on the mathematics section of the SAT, you might not be able to interpret exactly what that score represented. If a test were based on a measurement scale that ranged from a minimum low score of 0 to a maximum high score of 100, however, you might find the result more familiar. As an analogy, the temperature of 72°F is the equivalent of 22.22°C. Most Americans are more familiar with measuring temperature with the Fahrenheit scale; the Celsius system can be confusing unless you are a scientist who uses the Celsius scale in your work. In the field of education, we work with numerical measurements, reported as scores that are assigned to one of four types of measurement scales—*ordinal, nominal, interval, or ratio.*

MEASUREMENT SCALES

Ordinal Scales. *Ordinal scales* classify numbers into a set in which each number is either less than, equal to, or greater than every other number. Ordinal scales imply an ordered number sequence. For example, a teacher may take height measurements and arrange students in order from the tallest to the shortest student. In a similar fashion, the marks on examinations can be put in order from the lowest score to the highest score. It is important that, as a teacher, you understand how to interpret data, because misinterpretation or misuse of statistics can be misleading. For example, if you were to rank order the members of a professional basketball team from tallest to shortest, the results should not be interpreted to mean that the shortest player at 6'5" is "short." Such an assumption would be misleading. Similarly, a student who has the lowest math score in a gifted class is not necessarily a poor math student.

Nominal Scales. *Nominal scales* classify numbers into different (named) categories. For example, a teacher might use a nominal scale to assign students into two different groups on the basis of gender. On this basis, the teacher might observe that, of 26 students, 12 male students scored 80% or higher on an exam, while 14 female students scored 80% or higher on the same examination.

Interval Scales. *Interval scales* classify numbers in equal units, but they do not have a true zero. Temperature is measured on an interval scale: A difference of 1 degree is always the same size. Most psychological tests use interval scales, and, because the scores represent equal units, they can be added or subtracted. Thus, a student whose IQ is 120 can be said to have an IQ that is 20 points higher than one whose IQ is 100. Because IQ measurement does not have a true zero, however, we cannot say that an IQ of 120 is twice as high as an IQ of 60. In actual mental capability, a score of 120 is probably much more than twice a score of 60.

WHY IS FREEZING 32°?

My favorite example of the interval scale is the Fahrenheit temperature scale. Have you ever wondered how Gabriel Fahrenheit arrived at 32° as the freezing point and 212° as the boiling point of water? Hint: Subtract the difference, and you get 180°, which in simple geometry, gives you the diameter of a circle (remember a circle has 360°). The point here is that Gabriel Fahrenheit selected his scale, which is an interval scale, arbitrarily.

Ratio Scales. The *ratio scale,* like the interval scale, is a classification of numbers expressed in equal units. However, unlike the interval scale, the ratio scale has a true zero. Some examples of the ratio scale are units of time, distance measurements on a ruler in inches, and the measurement of mass in grams, all of which are typically used in the physical sciences. All of these numbers can be multiplied and divided, as well as added and subtracted. A ratio scale is distinguished from an interval scale by the fact that it has a true zero (as in money), while an interval scale does not have a true zero (as in intelligence). Ratio scales, however, are rarely encountered in educational statistics, testing, and measurements.

VARIABLES

Variables are symbols that can take on a variety of numerical values. In statistics, many of the variables that we use are displayed either italicized or as Greek letters. In educational testing and measurement we use these variables to represent scores. For example, if x represents a set of test scores, x_1 is the first examinee's score, x_2 the second examinee's score, x_3 the third examinee's score, and so forth (see Table 2.1). In addition, there are two other types of variables, *discrete* and *continuous*, that relate to educational testing.

Table 2.1	
	X
x_1	87
x_2	93
x_3	65
x_4	78
x_5	87
x_6	99
x_7	75
x_8	68
x_9	65
x_{10}	88

Continuous Variables. A *continuous variable* is a variable that can be divided into an infinite number of fractional parts. For example, time is a continuous variable because an infinite number of possible values falls between any two observations (see Figure 2.1.). In education, we most often work with continuous variables from the interval measurement scales.

Figure 2.1

Continuous Variable

Time in Minutes

10:25............................12:50............................14:75

10................11................12................13................14................15

Time in Hours

Discrete Variables. A *discrete variable* cannot be divided into fractional parts. Some examples are class size, family size, gender, or the combined value of rolling dice. Gender, for example, observes males and females, two values that cannot be divided into fractional parts. Thus, gender is a discrete variable.

IQs, however, are numerical values that arbitrarily range from 25 and below, indicating profound mental retardation, to 130 and above, which indicates a very superior intelligence. Unlike the example of time, however, IQs increase by increments of one unit (i.e., 100, 101, 102, and so forth) along a cognitive ability continuum. Therefore, IQs are not reported as continuous variables (scores such as 100.53 and 112.52).

In this section, we have seen how numbers are categorized into different scales of measurement, continuous variables, and discrete variables. Now we move on to the subject of data organization. We will see that teachers can arrange test data so that they can be organized and interpreted descriptively through the design of statistical graphs.

ORGANIZING AND ARRANGING DATA

Frequency Distributions. After collecting test results, teachers need to organize and arrange test data into a systematic numerical arrangement. First, you should begin data organization by arranging the numbers in order, which is called an array. For example, as a science teacher, you administer a test to 23 students ($n = 23$). The students' scores on the test are shown in Table 2.2.

The next step is to organize these test results so that they are more understandable. You do this by arranging the scores from the highest to the lowest (see Table 2.3). This pattern is the array. An array makes it simple for you to visualize the entire range, or distribution, of scores.

Table 2.2 Science Test Results	Table 2.3 An Array for Science Test Results
77	100
77	98
67	97
65	90
97	89
90	89
89	89
89	89
100	81
98	80
64	80
50	79
42	77
74	77
73	74
72	73
72	72
70	72
89	70
81	67
80	65
80	64
79	50
	42

Frequency Table. Once we have created an array, we can create a frequency table. A frequency expresses the frequency of occurrence. For example, a teacher can see how many students out of 20 obtained 75% of the possible grade on a social studies test. Frequency tables are useful when working with large distributions of numbers because they simplify data analysis by organizing the data. To create a frequency table from the array shown in Table 2.3, we tally the scores on the basis of each value's frequency (see Table 2.4). Each check mark indicates one appearance of a particular score in the array.

Table 2.4

Creating a Frequency Table From the Array Shown in Table 2.3

(1) Group the numbers	(2) Tally the numbers	(3) Determine the frequency
100	✓	1
98	✓	1
97	✓	1
90	✓	1
89, 89, 89	✓ ✓ ✓	3
81	✓	1
80, 80	✓ ✓	2
79	✓	1
77, 77	✓ ✓	2
74	✓	1
73	✓	1
72, 72	✓ ✓	2
70,	✓	1
67	✓	1
65	✓	1
64	✓	1
50	✓	1
42	✓	1

CHECK FOR UNDERSTANDING

2.1.   Create an array for the following test scores ($n = 20$): 89, 85, 80, 99, 98, 64, 50, 42, 90, 90, 90, 80, 79, 77, 77, 74, 73, 72, 70, 80.

2.2.   A questionnaire has items concerning (a) the number of elementary teachers in a school district, (b) the county in which the district is located, and (c) the district's rank on a recent statewide assessment tool.
Identify the scale of measurement (ordinal, nominal, interval, or ratio) used for each of the above pieces of data.

2.3.   Which scale would be used to determine the time in seconds that it takes for a student to complete a problem-solving exercise?

2.4.   Define the term *ordinal scale* and give an example of an ordinal scale that teachers may use.

Frequency Graphs. *Frequency graphs* present frequency distributions, which are a useful way to organize data into graphs and tables. First, to help you understand graphs, we should review the basic algebraic principles that apply to the graphical presentation of data. You probably recall that when graphing or plotting is done with reference to two lines (which are referred to as *coordinate axes*) the horizontal axis is known as the *x*-axis and the vertical axis is called the *y*-axis. These basic lines are perpendicular to each other. Figure 2.2 represents a system of coordinate axes, and Figure 2.3 shows how these axes would be arranged on a *Cartesian grid* (named for the French philosopher Rene Descartes). You may be familiar with the Cartesian grid example found in Figure 2.3, which shows *x*- and *y*-axes that range from negative to positive values.

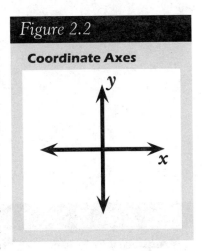

Figure 2.2

Coordinate Axes

The first type of statistical graph that we will discuss is the frequency polygon, a type of line graph that shows the frequency of each data point. Figure 2.4 is an example of a frequency polygon.

The second type of statistical graph that we will examine is the histogram, which is a type of bar graph. The width of each bar covers the numerical value of the scores. This type of graph is illustrated in Figure 2.5.

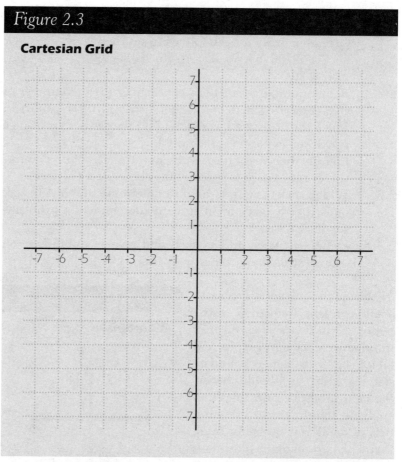

Figure 2.3

Cartesian Grid

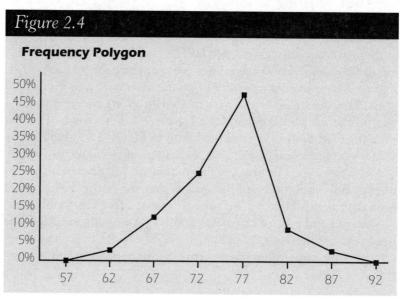

Figure 2.4

Frequency Polygon

Figure 2.5

Histogram

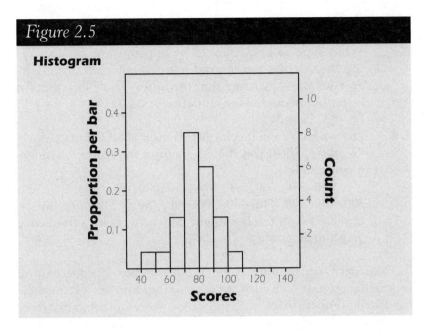

The next graph we look at is a simple bar graph, a statistical graph that is typically used when a frequency distribution is displaying data from nominal or ordinal data scales. This type of graph is illustrated in Figure 2.6. Note that the height of each bar corresponds to the frequency of the numerical value.

Figure 2.6

Bar Graph

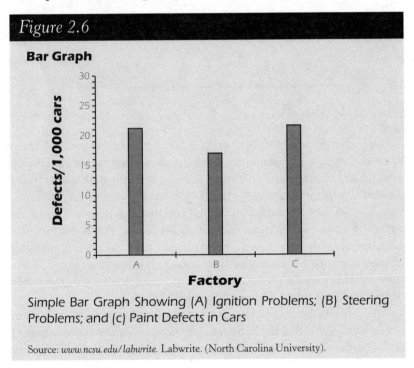

Simple Bar Graph Showing (A) Ignition Problems; (B) Steering Problems; and (c) Paint Defects in Cars

Source: *www.ncsu.edu/labwrite*. Labwrite. (North Carolina University).

CHECK FOR UNDERSTANDING

2.5.   What type of graph would be appropriate for displaying the distribution of grades for 20 students in a mathematics class? Assume that the letter-grade distribution
is the following for the students: As = 3, Bs = 5, Cs = 7,
Ds = 3, Fs = 2.

2.6.   Draw a bar graph for the distribution of SAT-I mathematics scores. Hint: You should organize the scores into a frequency table.
390, 600, 440, 700, 390, 600, 750, 600, 390, 500, 500, 500,
300, 700, 500, 440, 440, 500, 600, 780.

2.7.   Explain why a teacher might decide to create a frequency
graph to illustrate test results.

Normal Distributions. A *normal distribution* is a distribution
in which scores are concentrated close to the center of a symmetrical distribution of scores, with only a few scores at either extreme.
The normal distribution is often referred to as a *bell curve* because
of its shape (see Figure 2.7).

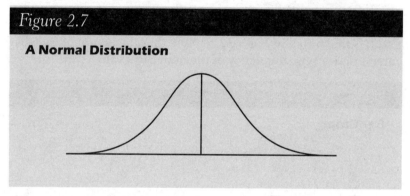

Figure 2.7

A Normal Distribution

All normal distribution graphs have the same general form
in that they are symmetrical, and the scores concentrate closely
around the center, taper off from the center high point, and move
toward the left and the right bases. Observe that the extreme left,
which is known as the left tail, has relatively few scores; and, as
we move to the right, toward what is known as the right tail, the
number of scores increases progressively to a maximum number
or frequency at the middle position. As we continue to move to the
right of the middle position, the number of scores progressively
decreases as we move nearer to the right tail.

An understanding of the characteristics of normal distribution
is essential for a teacher because IQ (e.g., Stanford-Binet Scale)
and standardized test scores (e.g., Iowa Tests of Basic Skills) are

THE BELL CURVE CONTROVERSY

In 1994, two Harvard University researchers, Richard Herrnstein and Charles Murray, wrote *The Bell Curve: Intelligence and Class Structure in American Life*. In this book, the authors found that intelligence level is related to social-class rank: People with high intelligence are more likely to occupy high social positions in occupations such as physician, lawyer, and professors. Herrnstein and Murray contend, for example, that the emergence of a "cognitive elite" class of individuals has transformed the social and economic boundaries of society and that people with high intelligence further their education and gravitate toward higher-paying jobs. In contrast, Herrnstein and Murray present a correlation between people with low intelligence and social problems such as school dropouts, high unemployment, domestic violence, out-of-wedlock births, work-related injury, and crime. In addition, the authors said that measured levels of intelligence differ among ethnic groups, and that Asian Americans, for example, score higher on IQ exams and have higher IQs than African Americans

In 1996, the late Steven Jay Gould, a well-known Harvard professor and science writer, responded to Herrnstein and Murray's book with the republication of his book *The Mismeasure of Man: The Definitive Refutation to the Argument of the Bell Curve*, in which he explores the history of intelligence theory from the late 1700s to the present. Gould argued that race and class differences cannot be explained by categorical classifications and IQ test scores alone. Gould's conclusion was that Herrnstein and Murray were prejudiced against the lower social classes of society. As you can see from this well-known case, it is essential that you understand that statistics can be misleading, misunderstood, and abused. With this understanding, you should accept the necessity of accurately interpreting all statistical representations.

normally distributed. Again, a normal distribution occurs when many scores are clustered in the middle and fewer scores fall within the tails, the outside limits of the normal distribution. An analogy of height and intelligence is helpful. Very few people are three feet tall or seven feet tall, and very few people have either extremely high intelligence or extremely low intelligence. Most people are somewhere in the middle of each of these categories—about 68% of all people fall in the middle of the normal distribution. More time will be dedicated to the discussion of the bell curve, also known as the normal curve, in subsequent chapters.

Skewed Distributions. Sometimes a distribution will have more scores clustered at either the high or the low ends, which shifts the center of the distribution to one side or the other. When the scores are clustered at the high end of the scale, distributions are *negatively skewed*. The term *negatively* can be misleading because we generally associate *negative* with low and *positive* with high. In this instance, the associations are reversed. For example, if the majority of students receive As and Bs on a test, rather than Cs, Ds, or Fs, the distribution is negatively skewed. An example of a negatively skewed distribution is shown as the grade inflation of Figure 2.8.

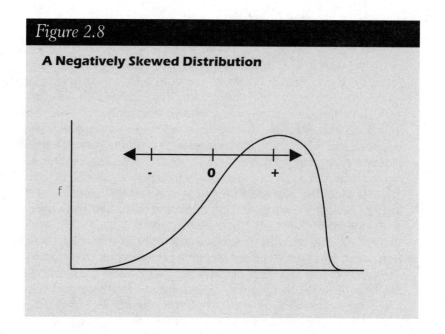

Figure 2.8

A Negatively Skewed Distribution

The opposite is a positively skewed distribution, which occurs when the scores are crowded together at the low end (or left) of the scale. An example of a *positively skewed* distribution of scores is income, because more people have low incomes than high income. An example of a positively skewed distribution is shown in Figure 2.9.

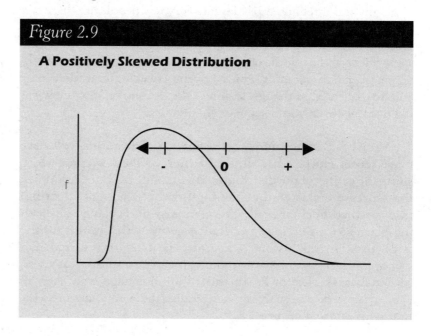

Figure 2.9

A Positively Skewed Distribution

This concept will be explained further in the next chapter, when we explore central tendency. In this next chapter, you will also gain an understanding of how the position of each of the three measures of central tendency (the mean, the median, and the mode) changes from being at the same point in a normal distribution, to different levels or points in a skewed distribution.

CHECK FOR UNDERSTANDING

2.8.   Explain a classroom scenario in which a negatively skewed distribution of grades would be likely.

2.9.   Draw (1) a normal distribution, (2) a negatively skewed distribution, and (3) a positively skewed distribution.

2.10.   If we had height measurements for every adult in the United States and plotted a curve with all of the data, would the distribution be normal or skewed?

ROUNDING NUMBERS

When performing statistical calculations, you determine the level of accuracy necessary for the problem. For example, scientists will sometimes carry their figures to four decimal places—88.6783, for example. If rounded to two decimal places, this figure would become 88.68, and to one decimal, 88.7. For the most part, at least for the subsequent problems that you will encounter in this book, you and all educators should use a system for rounding numbers to two decimals. A suggestion for rounding to two decimals: When the third decimal is less than five, the second decimal does not change—74.983 becomes 74.98. When the third decimal is 5 or greater, the second decimal is increased by one—86.768 becomes 86.77 and 86.764 becomes 86.76.

IN SUMMARY

There are four different scales of measurement: ordinal, nominal, interval, and ratio. In educational statistics, we most often examine numerical data from the perspective of interval scales of measurement. An ordinal scale, for example, can show class rankings; a nominal scale is appropriate for dividing students according to gender; an interval scale can show the distribution of test scores; and a ratio scale can be used to illustrate the components of time. A continuous variable can be divided into an infinite number of fractional parts, whereas a discrete variable is not divisible. For example, temperature and money are continuous variables, while IQs are discrete variables because they are not divisible.

Descriptive statistics provide the basis for portraying data distributions through graphics such as histograms, bar graphs, and frequency polygons. A normal distribution of data is seen as symmetrical, but when the data are clustered at one end or the other, the distribution is skewed.

CHAPTER REVIEW QUESTIONS

2.11. If a teacher arranges grades from highest to lowest, what scale of measurement is being used?

2.12. Organize the following test scores into a frequency array. 75, 100, 67, 88, 74, 91, 55, 100, 67, 74, 77, 82, 87, 94, 66, 71, 75, 84, 91, and 82.

2.13. Using the frequency array that you made in problem 2.12, create a frequency table.

2.14. AND 2.15. The following table is for questions 2.14 and 2.15.

X	Frequency
97	1
86	2
84	1
75	3
74	1
68	1

2.14. For these data, $n =$ ___.
a. 5
b. 6
c. 9
d. cannot be determined.

2.15. For the set of data presented above, draw a histogram.

2.16. What is the shape of the distribution for the following set of test scores?
40, 50, 60, 60, 70, 70, 70, 80, 80, 90, 100
a. positively skewed
b. negatively skewed
c. symmetrical
d. cannot be determined

Questions 2.17, 2.18, and 2.19 refer to the following graph showing a distribution of test scores

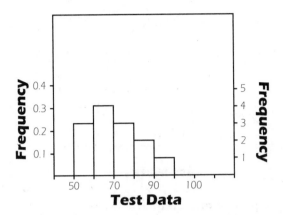

2.17.   This is an example of a _____ distribution?
        a. positively skewed
        b. negatively skewed
        c. symmetrical
        d. cannot be determined

2.18.   Based on the individual scores represented in this graph,
        how many students took the test? (What is the value of n?)
        a. 13
        b. 4
        c. 5
        d. cannot be determined

2.19.   For this set of exam scores, how many students scored
        under 70?
        a. 10
        b. 5
        c. 7
        d. cannot be determined

The following graph is for question 2.20.

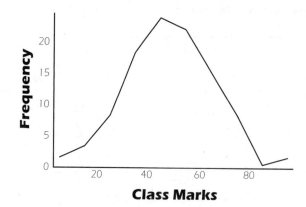

2.20. This graph is an example of a _____?
a. histogram
b. frequency polygon
c. bar graph
d. none of the above

ANSWERS: CHECK FOR UNDERSTANDING

2.1. 99, 98, 90, 90, 90, 89, 85, 80, 80, 80, 79, 77, 77, 74, 73, 72, 70, 64, 50, 42.

2.2 a. ratio
b. nominal
c. ordinal

2.3. A continuous variable.

2.4. An ordinal measurement assigns higher numbers to individuals who score higher on a test. The most common type of ordinal measurement is rank order. For example, a teacher might organize test scores from the highest score to the lowest. The higher the test score, the higher the rank.

2.5. A bar chart because the data scale is nominal.

2.6.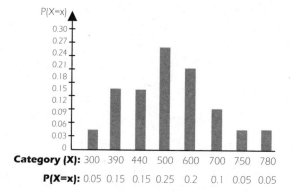

2.7. By organizing and simplifying your data into a graph, you condense them into a comprehensible snapshot.

2.8. A gifted or advanced placement class because the students are of above average aptitude and/or cognitive ability.

2.9.

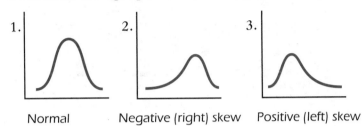

Normal   Negative (right) skew   Positive (left) skew

2.10. A normal distribution. Since we have an entire population, this distribution would be normal.

ANSWERS: CHAPTER REVIEW QUESTIONS

2.11. Ordinal

2.12. 100, 100, 94, 91, 91, 88, 87, 84, 82, 82, 77, 75, 75, 74, 74, 71, 67, 67, 66, 55

2.13.

X	frequency
100	2
94	1
91	2
88	1
87	1
84	1
82	2
77	1
75	2
74	2
71	1
67	2
66	1
55	1

2.14. c. 9

2.15.

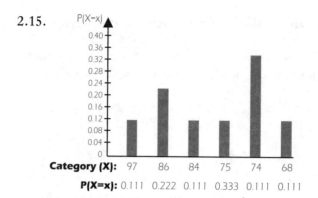

Category (X):	97	86	84	75	74	68
P(X=x):	0.111	0.222	0.111	0.333	0.111	0.111

2.16. c. symmetrical
2.17. a. positively skewed
2.18. a. 13
2.19. c. 7
2.20. b. frequency polygon

CALCULATOR EXPLORATION

Using the TI-73, TI-83, or TI-84 graphing calculator, you can easily sort numbers by following these keystrokes.

TI-73

Step 1. Display list editor by pressing [LIST]. Under L1under Science Test Results in Table 2.3.

L1	L2	L3	1
100	------	------	
98			
97			
90			
89			
89			
89			

L1(1)=100

Step 2. Press 2nd [LIST] to activate STAT. Next, scroll to the right and select OPS. Next, scroll down to 1: Sort A, press [1], then press ENTER.

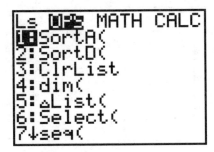

Step 3. After the [SortA(] is available, press 2nd [LIST] to activate [STAT]. Next, press 1, then press [)], and press [ENTER].

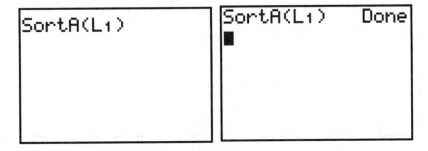

Step 4. Press [List] to get the variables listed from lowest to highest.

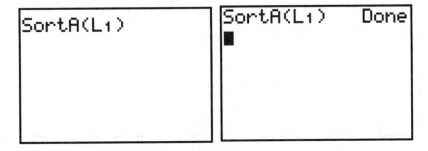

TI-83/TI-84

Step 1. First press [STAT]. Next, select 1:Edit by pressing 1. Here you can enter up to 999 elements.

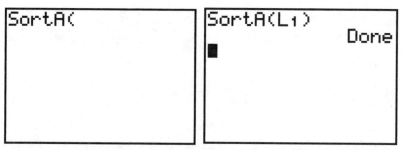

Step 2. Press [STAT] and scroll down to Sort A (Next, activate the 2nd function, press L1, and press [)], which is above the 9. Next press ENTER.

Step 3. Press [LIST]. Next, scroll down to 1: L1 and press 1. Next, press enter to get the numbers listed in order from lowest to highest.

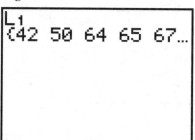

INTERNET RESOURCES

http://nces.ed.gov

This site of the National Center for Educational Statistics provides a kaleidoscope of statistics related to national and international performance in education. For example, How many schools have access to the internet? Which state scores the highest on the NAEP test?

www.nea.org/edstats

The National Education Association website offers statistics related to education. Graphic displays include data on teacher salaries, public school enrollment, and expenditures on education.

http://math.about.com/cs/statistics

This site offers helpful suggestions for the understanding and appropriate implementation of elementary statistical calculations.

REFERENCES

Allen, M. J., and W. M. Yen. 2002. *Introduction to measurement theory.* Chicago: Waveland.

Gould, S. J. 1996. *The mismeasure of man: The definitive refutation to the argument of the bell curve.* New York: W. W. Norton.

Herrnstein, R. J., and C. Murray. 1994. *The bell curve: Intelligence and class structure in American life.* New York: Free Press.

FURTHER READING

Christmann, E. P. 2002. Graphing calculators. *Science Scope* 25 (5): 46–48.

Christmann, E. P., and J. L. Badgett. 2001. A comparative analysis of the academic performances of elementary education pre-professionals, as disclosed by four methods of assessment. *Mid-Western Educational Researcher* 14 (2): 32–36.

Christmann, E. P., and J. L. Badgett. 1999. The comparative effectiveness of various microcomputer-based software packages on statistics achievement. *Computers in the Schools* 16 (1): 209–220.

Elmore, P. B., and P. L. Woehlke. 1997. *Basic statistics.* New York: Longman.

Gravetter, F. J., and L. B. Wallnau. 2002. *Essentials of statistics for the behavioral sciences.* New York: West.

Raymondu, J. C. 1999. *Statistical analysis in the behavioral sciences.* New York: McGraw-Hill.

Thorne, B. M., and J. M. Giesen. 2000. *Statistics for the behavioral sciences.* Mountain View, CA: Mayfield.

Zawojewski, J. S., and J. M. Shaughnessy. 2000. Mean and median: Are they really so easy? *Mathematics Teaching in the Middle School* 57: 436–440.

Chapter 3

CENTRAL TENDENCY AND VARIABILITY

OBJECTIVES

When you complete this chapter, you should be able to
1. formulate questions that can be addressed with data and collect, organize, and display relevant data to answer them;
2. use measures of central tendency, focusing on the mean, median, and mode;
3. describe the shape and important features of a set of data and compare related data sets, with an emphasis on how the data are distributed;
4. select and use appropriate statistical methods to calculate standard deviation; and
5. compare different representations of the same data and evaluate how well each representation shows important aspects of the data.

Key Terms

When you complete this chapter, you should be able to understand

central tendency	range
heterogeneous group	sample standard deviation
homogeneous group	skewed distribution
mean	standard deviation
median	variation
mode	variability
normal distribution	variance
outlier	

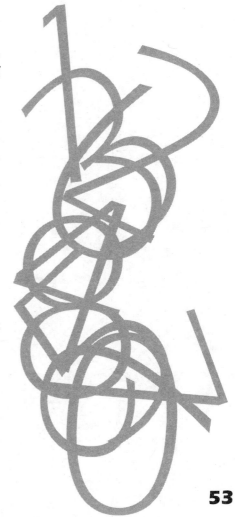

This chapter presents two important interrelated topics in statistics: central tendency and variability. Measures of *central tendency* show how similar the data points in a set of data are, while measures of *variability* show how much the data points vary. Central tendency calculations determine representative scores within a distribution (see Chapter 2). For example, in a set of test scores consisting of 82, 86, 90, 94, and 98, the central score, 90, is the most representative of all the scores. The difference between the highest and lowest scores, 16, shows how much the scores vary. Variability shows how "scattered" or "spread out" the scores are around the center point of the distribution. In the first half of this chapter we will discuss three important measures of central tendency, the *mean, median,* and *mode*. In the second half, we will cover three measures of variation, the *range, standard deviation,* and *variance*.

Both central tendency and variation have important practical uses for teachers. For example, suppose you administered a 100-point science test to two classes of 25 students each (see Table 3.1). Based on the scores reported in Table 3.1, the average, or mean score for Class A is 77.12 ($n = 25$), and the mean score for Class B is also 77.12 ($n = 25$). Because the average scores are identical, you might assume that there is no difference between the two groups. If you examine variability as well as central tendency, however, you immediately see an important difference. For example, Class A's scores range from a low of 0 to a high of 100, while Class B's range from a low of 70 to a high of 84. Clearly, Class A's scores are more spread out, or have more variation.

Because Class A's scores have such high variation, the class is probably a group of mixed abilities. Groups of mixed ability are *heterogeneous*. In contrast, Class B's scores fall around the same point in the scale, reflecting a more similar range of ability. Groups that are of similar ability are *homogeneous*. The difference in variability would be important to you as a teacher, because you would need to use different instructional strategies with each group.

Table 3.1

Science Test Results

Class A	Class B
100	84
99	83
98	82
98	81
97	80
94	80
93	79
88	79
87	78
86	78
85	78
80	77
79	77
78	77
77	77
75	76
74	76
70	76
69	75
67	75
66	74
65	73
54	72
49	71
0	70

CENTRAL TENDENCY

This section presents the three measures of *central tendency:* the *mean,* the *median,* and the *mode.* A measure of central tendency is a value that is representative of a data set. In a normal distribution of scores (see Chapter 2), all measures of central tendency would fall precisely at the same point, which is the line located exactly in the middle of the bell curve (see Figure 3.1.) Measures of central tendency are useful for summarizing a large set of scores in a meaningful way. We read and hear these terms all the time in the media:

• The *mean* is the average value of all the data in the set.
• The *median* is the value that has exactly half the data above it and half below it.
• The *mode* is the value that occurs most frequently in the set.

SOME COMMON MEASURES OF CENTRAL TENDENCY FOUND IN THE MEDIA

• Average Teacher Salary in the United States: $45,930
(NEA Research, Estimates databank, Fall 2003)

• U.S. median household income: $42,228
(U.S. Census Bureau, 2002)

• Average household net worth of the top 1% of wage earners: $10,204,000
Average net worth of the bottom 40% of wage earners: $1,900
(Edward N. Wolff, "Recent Trends in Wealth Ownership, 1983-1998," April 2000)

• Definition of middle class in terms of mean annual income: $32,653 to $48,979
(Economy.Com's The Dismal Scientist, 1999)

• Median hourly wage of a former welfare recipient: $6.61
(Urban Institute, 2000)

• Bill Gates's average hourly wage: $650,000/hr
(Bill Gates's Net Worth Page, average since 1986)

• Average teacher salaries
U.S. average: $45,930
California: $56,283 (highest)
South Dakota: $32,416 (lowest)
(NEA estimates for 2003)

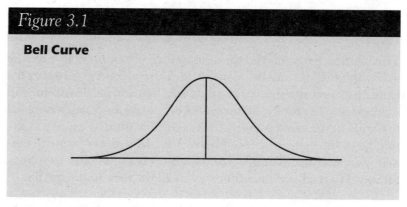

Figure 3.1

Bell Curve

The Mean

The most common measure of central tendency is the *mean,* which is the arithmetic average of a set of scores. To compute the mean from a set of numbers, add them, then divide their sum, Σx, by the total number of values, n (see Table 3.2 for the definitions of Σ and other symbols). For example, if a student has obtained scores of 16, 18, and 17 on three math quizzes, the student's mean, or average score is 17. The symbol $\bar{x}$, which represents the sample mean, will be used in most cases to represent the mean in this text. The procedure is illustrated in Equation 3.1.

Equation 3.1

$$\bar{x} = \frac{\Sigma x}{n}$$

Table 3.2

Symbols Used to Compute Measures of Central Tendency

Σ	The summation of a set of values
x	The variable that represents the individual data values
n	The number of values in a sample
N	The number of values in a population
$\bar{x}$	The mean of a set of sample values
Md	The median of a set of sample values
μ	The mean of all of the values in a population
s	The standard deviation of a set of sample values

For example, you might administer a quiz to a small class of 10 students. If x represents an individual test result, and $x_1 = 96$, $x_2 = 96$, $x_3 = 87$, $x_4 = 84$, $x_5 = 79$, $x_6 = 75$, $x_7 = 72$, $x_8 = 68$, $x_9 = 65$, $x_{10} = 55$, then the sum of the $n = 10$ scores is $\Sigma x = 96 + 96 + 87 + 84 + 79 + 75 + 72 + 68 + 65 + 55 = 777$. Thus, the calculation of the mean, $\bar{x}$, using equation 3.1, is $777/10 = 77.70$.

Because the mean takes into account the value of each score, one extremely low or high score can affect its value. For example, recall the student who scored 16, 18, and 17 on three math quizzes. If she scored a 2 on a fourth quiz, her mean score would decrease from 17 to 13.25. The mean is very sensitive to extreme measures, so it is not the best measure of central tendency to use in all cases.

CHECK FOR UNDERSTANDING

3.1. Compute the mean for the following distribution of test scores: 100, 98, 97, 90, 89, 89, 85, 81, 80, 80, 79, 77, 77, 74, 73, 72, 72, 70, 67, 65, 64, 50, 42.

3.2. Add 5 points to each test score from 3.1 and compute the mean again. How did adding 5 points to each score affect the mean?

3.3. Add 10% to each score from 3.1. Explain what happened to the mean. Is there a difference between adding or subtracting from each score? Is there a difference between multiplying or dividing each score by a percentage?

The Median

The *median* of a set of scores is the value that divides the scores into equal halves. To return to the same simple example we used for the mean, if a student scores 16, 18, and 17 on three math quizzes, the student's median score is 17. To calculate a median, arrange the scores in rank order. The middle score is the median. For example, suppose a group of students obtains the following scores on a social studies quiz: 100, 94, 87, 85, 85, 79, 75, 71, 62. The median is the score that lies in the middle, 85 (Md = 85). For a distribution with an even number of scores (such as 95, 93, 88, 86, 77, 70), the median is halfway between the two middle values. It is calculated by averaging the two middle values (see Equation 3.2).

Equation 3.2

$$Md = \frac{88 + 86}{2} = 87$$

The median is most properly used when the distribution is skewed, or not arranged in a normal distribution (see Chapter 2). Unlike the mean, the median is not sensitive to an extremely high or extremely low score. Therefore, the median is a better way than the mean to describe this distribution. For example, assume that you wanted to compute the mean annual income of this particular class. A new student enrolls in the class. His name is Bill—Bill Gates. We find that the mean annual income of your class is now in the millions. But Bill Gates' income would not drastically change the median, so the median would give you a much more accurate idea of your class's average annual income.

CHECK FOR UNDERSTANDING

3.4. Find the median for the following set of test scores: 100, 95, 93, 88, 86, 80, 77, 75, 70, 65.

3.5. Find the median for the following set of test scores (note: first arrange the scores in order from highest to lowest): 74, 100, 95, 86, 71, 74, 65, 55, 84.

3.6. Calculate the mean and median for the following test scores: 71, 100, 100, 98, 97, 99, 100, 88, 87, 10.

3.7. Which measure of central tendency better represents the distribution of scores, the mean or the median? Explain your answer.

The Mode

The *mode* is the score that occurs most frequently in a distribution. For example, if a student obtained scores of 97, 94, 88, 88, 80, 74, and 50 on spelling tests, the mode is 88, because this score occurs twice, which is more often than any of the student's other scores. A set of scores may have no mode, or it may have more than one mode. A distribution with two modes is called a *bimodal distribution*. For example, the following numbers represent quiz scores for an eighth-grade science class: 10, 10, 9, 9, 9, 8, 8, 8, 8, 7, 7, 7, 7, 6, 5, 3. This distribution is bimodal. The scores 7 and 8 both appear four times.

For this set of scores, the mean is 7.56 and the median is 8 (see Calculation 3.1). Thus, you can now see how all three measures of central tendency assist in the description of data. Because

---

Calculation 3.1

$$Md = \frac{8 + 8}{2} = 8$$

---

the median exceeds the mean in this set of scores, it is apparent that the distribution is negatively skewed (see Figure 3.2). As a teacher, for example, you should know that, contrary to what the term may imply, a negatively skewed distribution has more As and Bs than Ds and Fs. In contrast, a positively skewed distribution has more Ds and Fs than As and Bs. Remember, a negatively skewed distribution has more higher than lower scores, whereas a positively skewed distribution has more lower than higher scores. It is not unusual that a gifted class would have a negatively skewed distribution of test scores because the class comprises students with above average ability.

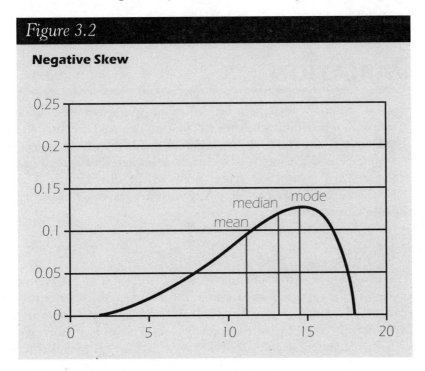

Figure 3.2

Negative Skew

CHECK FOR UNDERSTANDING

Use the following distribution of test scores for questions 3.8 through 3.10: 95, 92, 92, 88, 85, 85, 85, 80, 77, 75, 75, 59.

3.8.   What is the value of the mode?

3.9.   What is the value of n? Calculate the mean and the median.

3.10.   Describe the shape of the distribution.

IS YOUR EDUCATION WORTH THE INVESTMENT?

- Median household income for those with less than a 9th-grade education: $17,261
- Median household income for those with a 9th- through 12th-grade education (no diploma): $21,737
- Median household income for high school graduates: $35,744
- Median household income for college graduates with a BA: $64,406
- Median household income for college graduates with an MA: $74,476
- Median household income for professional degree holders: $100,000

(U.S. Census Bureau, 1999)

VARIATION

Central tendency calculations help determine representative values of scores in a distribution. After calculating central tendency, the next step is to determine the *variation* of the distribution's scores. Variation provides a way to measure how scattered or spread out the scores are around the center point of the distribution. The three measures of variation we will discuss are the *range, standard deviation,* and *variance.*

Range

The *range* is the difference between the highest and the lowest scores in a data set. For an example, refer back to the science test scores for two classes given in Table 3.1. To calculate the range of scores in Class A, we subtract 0 from 100 and get a range of 100 (see Calculation 3.2). Likewise, for Class B we subtract 70 from 84 and arrive at a range of 14 (see Calculation 3.3). As you see, the range is a simple way to describe how spread out the scores are. Because the range does not take into account all of the scores in the distribution and is sensitive to extremely

---

Calculation 3.2

Range = 100 − 0 = 100

Calculation 3.3

Range = 84 − 70 = 14

---

high and extremely low scores, it is not the most reliable measurement of variation, as you also can see from Calculation 3.2 and Calculation 3.3. Consequently, we use the variance and the standard deviation to provide more reliable and truthful measurements of variability.

Standard Deviation and Variance

The *standard deviation* is the best statistic to use to determine the mathematical variation, or the amount of dispersion, among the scores in relation to the mean of a distribution. It shows how spread out the data are in a sample or a population. The standard deviation is the first step in the calculation of most other statistics. In this text, we will cover only the *sample standard deviation*, which is what is used for the small samples that classroom teachers typically work with.

When teachers work with standardized tests, however, they use norm-referenced data. When we speak of *norm-referenced data*, we are talking about comparisons among the units within a set of data, which could be a set of test scores. With this approach, an individual's test score is viewed in terms of how it compares with the other test scores. For example, if an individual scored in the 95th percentile, we mean that he or she scored as high as or higher than 95% of the people who took the same test. Even if this student answered only 38 of 100 items correctly, he or she could still score in the 95th percentile, depending on how the other students scored. This student's raw score of 38, however, is viewed as *criterion-referenced data,* which is the number or percentage of items answered correctly out of 100 test items.

A simple way of viewing these two types of data illustrations is to understand that with criterion-referenced data we are comparing scores, whereas with norm-referenced data we are comparing the performances of people.

With norm-referenced data, the standard deviation is a point on a normal curve. Figure 3.3 shows the standard deviation units within a normal curve. The two areas in the middle area represent one standard deviation, the two areas lying directly beside the two middle areas represent two standard deviations, and the two outermost areas represent three standard deviation units. This concept will be useful in our discussion of standard scores in the next chapter.

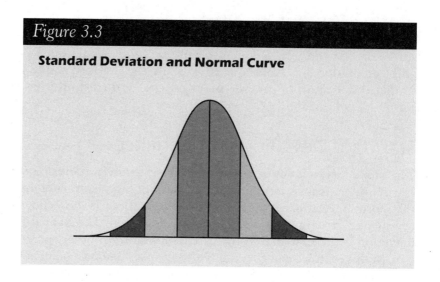

Figure 3.3

Standard Deviation and Normal Curve

Equation 3.4 shows the formula for calculating the sample standard deviation. In Table 3.2 we defined the symbol Σ, the upper-case Greek letter sigma, which means summation. (The lower-case sigma, σ, will be used as the symbol for population standard deviation. In this text, the symbol for sample standard deviation that will be used is the upper-case S.) Notice in Equation 3.5 that the sample standard deviation formula uses $n-1$ as the denominator in the formula. If you are wondering, $n-1$ is used as a mathematical method to correct for bias. It means that, if we have a small sample size, we will divide by a smaller number, which makes the product of the equation larger and thus allows the sample to reflect a less-biased estimate of the actual population.

Let's calculate the standard deviation of the scores for Class A in Table 3.1. First, we need to calculate the mean of this set of scores. Second, we calculate the deviation of each score from the mean: We subtract the mean from each score's value (x – mean). Notice, if we were to add all of the deviations, the sum would equal zero, because some scores would be larger and some smaller than the mean. Therefore, when the deviations are summed, they equal zero (see the bell curve in Figure 3.1). The third step is to square each deviation. The fourth step is to sum all of the squared scores. Calculation 3.4 shows the calculation of the standard deviation for the scores of Class A shown in Table 3.1. Then, the fifth step is to divide the sum of the squared scores, i.e., Σ (X – mean)^2 by $n-1$.

The resulting value is the average of the squares of the deviation, also known as the *variance* (see Equation 3.3). Like standard deviation, the variance is used to explain how scores are differ-

Calculation 3.4

Class A Scores X	Deviation (X – mean)	Squared Deviation (X – mean)^2
100.000	22.880	523.494
99.000	21.880	478.734
98.000	20.880	435.974
98.000	20.880	435.974
97.000	19.880	395.214
94.000	16.880	284.934
93.000	15.880	252.174
88.000	10.880	118.374
87.000	9.880	97.614
86.000	8.880	78.854
85.000	7.880	62.094
80.000	2.880	8.294
79.000	1.880	3.534
78.000	0.880	0.774
77.000	-0.120	0.014
75.000	-2.120	4.494
74.000	-3.120	9.734
70.000	-7.120	50.694
69.000	-8.120	65.934
67.000	-10.120	102.414
66.000	-11.120	123.650
65.000	-12.120	146.894
54.000	-23.120	534.534
49.000	-28.120	790.734
.000	-77.120	5947.494
Mean = 77.120	Σ(X – mean) = 0	Σ(X – mean)^2 = 10952.626

ent from one another. The variance, however, is a squared value. Therefore, the sixth and final step is to calculate the sample standard deviation, which is easily calculated by taking the square root of the variance (see Equation 3.4).

Equation 3.3

S^2 = Variance

$$S^2 = \frac{\Sigma\,(X - mean)^2}{n - 1}$$

Or

$$S^2 = \frac{10952.626}{24} = 456.359$$

> **Equation 3.4**
>
> S = Standard Deviation = $\sqrt{\text{variance}}$
>
> Or $S = \sqrt{456.359} = 21.363$

Another method used to calculate sample standard deviation is the computational formula. The computational formula is easier to calculate with a basic handheld calculator (see Equation 3.5). The following is a six-step guide to calculating sample standard deviation with the computational formula (see Table 3.3).

> **Equation 3.5**
>
> $$S = \sqrt{\frac{\Sigma X^2 - (\Sigma X)^2/n}{n-1}}$$
>
> Where
>
> ΣX^2 = The sum of the squared scores.
>
> $(\Sigma X)^2$ = The square of the sum of all of the scores.
>
> n = The total number of scores used in the computation.

Table 3.3

Computational Formula for Standard Deviation of the Science Test Results for Class A

Step 1. Add all of the scores.
$100.000 + 99.000 + 98.000 \ldots + 0.000 = 1928.000$

Step 2. Square each score and add all of the squared values.
$100.000^2 + 99.000^2 + 98.000^2 + \ldots 0.000^2 = 159640.000$

Step 3. Square the sum from Step 1 and divide by the total number of students in the class.
$1928.000^2/25 = 3717184/25 = 148687.360$

Step 4. Subtract the value obtained in Step 3 from the value in Step 2.
$159640.000 - 148687.360 = 10952.640$

Step 5. Divide the value calculated in Step 4 by n – 1, which gives us the variance.
$S^2 = 10952.640/24 = 456.360$

Step 6. Take the square root of the variance that was calculated in Step 5. This is the sample standard deviation.

$S = \sqrt{456.359} = 21.363$

Used together, the mean and the standard deviation can give you a good idea of how students performed on a test. For example, if you know that your students have a mean score of 70 on a mathematics test and the standard deviation is 10, you can estimate that about 68% of the students scored between 60 and 80 on the test and about 95% of the students earned scores between 50 and 90 on this exam.

This is because the normal distribution is based on the standard deviation in the following way: In any normal distribution of test scores, approximately 68% of the test scores fall within one standard deviation of the mean, 95% of the test scores fall within two standard deviations of the mean, and 99.9% of the test scores fall within three standard deviations of the mean (see Figure 3.4). In the class whose scores we have been examining, however, we have a relatively high standard deviation of 21.363. This is because of the single score of zero on the test. A single score that is located far from the rest of the data is called an *outlier*. As a general rule, outliers should be investigated. If, for example, the student who scored a zero on the test received the zero because he was absent on the day of the test, this score should not be included in the data set. Subsequently, for the remaining 24 scores the removal of the zero changes our standard deviation to from 21.363 to 14.382 and the mean from 77.120 to a 79.522. Now our test results are a better reflection of those students who took the test with approximately 68% of the 24 scores within one standard deviation of the mean. Note, however, that if a student took the test and scored a zero, that score should be included among the results.

The following example will further illustrate the usefulness of the standard deviation.

Assume that we have the following test scores from two sets of students:

Group A	Group B
50	50
50	40
50	60
50	70
50	30

The mean scores of the two groups is the same, but their standard deviations are quite different.

CHECK FOR UNDERSTANDING

3.11. What is the relationship between the standard deviation and variance?

Interpreting Assessment Data   **65**

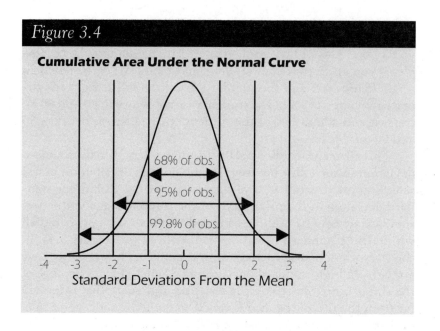

Figure 3.4

Cumulative Area Under the Normal Curve

68% of obs.

95% of obs.

99.8% of obs.

Standard Deviations From the Mean

3.12. Calculate the range, variance, and standard deviation for Class B's science test results from Table 3.1.

3.13. For the sample of scores 5, 2, 5, 4, calculate the range, variance, and standard deviation.

IN SUMMARY

There are three standard measures of central tendency. In most situations, the mean, or arithmetic average, is the most commonly used measure of central tendency. The median is the exact middle point of a distribution. In a perfect normal distribution, shown in Figure 3.4, the mean, median, and mode all have the same value. In a skewed distribution, however, the mean value does not correspond with the other two measures of central tendency. As the "balance point," the mean is pulled toward the drawn-out tail of the skewed distribution.

The mode is the most frequently occurring score, and it is the least useful measure of central tendency when the mean or median can be used. The mode, however, tells us the score with the highest frequency.

The range, the standard deviation, and its square, the variance, are used to illustrate the spread, or variability, of a group of scores. The range is the measure of variability that shows the spread of the scores and informs a teacher of whether or not the test results include extreme scores.

CHAPTER REVIEW QUESTIONS

3.14. What is the value of the mean for the following set of test scores? Test Scores: 100, 97, 93, 88, 84, 79, 75, 72, 68, 62, 50, and 0.
a. 85.50
b. 83.00
c. 71.44
d. 72.33

3.15. What is the value of the median for the following set of test scores? Test Scores: 100, 97, 93, 88, 84, 79, 75, 72, 68, 62, 50, and 0.
a. 75.00
b. 79.00
c. 78.50
d. 77.00

3.16. What is the value of the mode for the following set of test scores? Test Scores: 100, 97, 93, 88, 84, 79, 75, 72, 68, 62, 50, and 0.
a. 84.00
b. 79.00
c. 79.00 and 75.00
d. There is not a mode in this distribution of test grades.

3.17. Define and compare the three measures of central tendency.

3.18. Mrs. Smith's science class obtained the following scores on the Stanford Achievement Test: 100, 98, 97, 89, 89, 85, 82, 78, 77, 75, 75, 75, 68, 65, 60, 59, 30.
Determine the following:
a. $n =$
b. $\Sigma x =$
c. $\bar{x} =$
d. median =
e. mode =

3.19. through 3.23 Match the characteristics listed in Column A with the terms in Column B. The options in Column B may be used more than once.

Column A	Column B
_____ 3.19. the score that half of the examinees score at or below	a. mean
	b. median
_____ 3.20. the arithmetic average of scores	c. mode
_____ 3.21. the most frequently occurring score	
_____ 3.22. also known as the 50th percentile.	
_____ 3.23. more than one possible in the same distribution	

3.24.   For the set of test scores —100, 100, 98, 92, 90, 88, 84, 84, 84, 84, 76, 72, 66, 60, 55, 0, compute the following measurements:
a. $n =$
b. mean =
c. median =
d. mode =
e. range =
f. variance =
g. standard deviation =

3.25.   What statistical term do we use to describe how spread out or dispersed scores are within a distribution?

3.26.   If a distribution of test scores has a small standard deviation with a compressed appearance, it is known as which type of group?
a. Symmetrical group
b. Homogeneous group
c. Heterogeneous group
d. Similar group

3.27.   Define and compare the three major indicators of variability.

3.28.   Which set of test scores has the highest variability?
a. 77, 79, 82, 88
b. 65, 75, 85, 95
c. 70, 80, 90, 100
d. 0, 40, 60, 100

3.29.   To compute the sample variance, the sum of the squares is divided by _____?
a. $n - 1$
b. N
c. n
d. $\sqrt{n - 1}$

3.30.   The sample standard deviation is identified by which of the following symbols?
a. S^2
b. x
c. S
d. N

3.31.   Determine the range from the following set of test scores: 87, 76, 43, 97, 99

3.32.   Calculate the standard deviation and variance from the following set of test scores: 100, 99, 90, 99, 100.

3.33.   Based on the calculated standard deviation from question 3.32, is the group of scores heterogeneous or homogeneous?

CHALLENGE QUESTIONS

3.34.   If the average (arithmetic mean) of five numbers is equal to the median of the numbers, what is one possible value of x if the five numbers are 10, 6, 10, 4, and x?

3.35.   Using the data from Class A's science test scores from Table 3.1, add 5 points to every score and then compute the mean, range, and standard deviation. How is the standard deviation affected when a constant is added to every score?

ANSWERS: CHECK FOR UNDERSTANDING

3.1.   Mean = 77.00, sum X = 1771.00, n = 23

3.2.   Mean = 82.00, sum X = 1886.00, n = 23
       If a constant is added to a score, the same constant will be added to the mean.

3.3.   Mean = 84.70, sum X = 1948.10, n = 23
       Multiplying by a constant value is a method for changing the scale of measurement. When every score is multiplied by a constant value, the mean changes along with the constant value.

3.4.   Median = $\dfrac{86 + 80}{2}$ = 83

3.5.   100, 95, 86, 84, 74, 74, 71, 65, 55
       Median = 74

3.6.   100, 100, 100, 99, 98, 97, 88, 87, 71, 10
       Mean = 85.0
       Median = 97.50

3.7.   Since the distribution is negatively skewed, the median of these scores would be the measure of central tendency that best depicts the distribution.

3.8.   Mode = 85

3.9. n = 12, mean = 82.33, median = 85.00

3.10. Because the median exceeds the mean, the distribution is negatively skewed.

3.11. Standard deviation is the square root of variance.

3.12. Range is 14.000.
       Variance is 12.524.
       Standard deviation is 3.339.

3.13. n = 4
       Range is 3.000.
       Variance is 2.000.
       Standard deviation is 1.414.

ANSWERS: CHAPTER REVIEW QUESTIONS

3.14.   d. 72.33

3.15.   d. 77.00

3.16.   d. There is not a mode in this distribution of test grades.

3.17.   The mean is the average value of all the data in the set.
The median is the value that has exactly half the data above it and half below it.
The mode is the value that occurs most frequently in the set.

3.18.   a. $n = 17$
b. $\Sigma x = 1302$
c. $\bar{x} = 76.59$
d. median = 77.00
e. mode = 75.00

3.19. through 3.23.

3.19.   b

3.20.   a

3.21.   c

3.22.   b

3.23.   c

3.24.   a. $n = 16$
b. mean = 77.06
c. median = 84.00
d. mode = 84.00
e. range = 100
f. variance = 603.68
g. standard deviation = 24.57

3.25.   Variation

3.26.   b. Homogeneous group

3.27.   The range is the difference between the highest and the lowest scores in a data set.

The standard deviation is the best statistic to use to determine the mathematical variation, or the amount of dispersion, among the scores in relation to the mean of a distribution.

The variance is the resulting value of the average of the squares of the deviation.

3.28.   d. 0, 40, 60, 100

3.29.   a. $n - 1$

3.30.   c. S

3.31.   Range = 56

3.32 .   Standard deviation = 23.04
Variance = 18.3

3.33.   More homogeneous

ANSWERS: CHALLENGE QUESTIONS

3.34. $x = 0$ or $x = 20$ or $x = 7.5$

3.35. $n = 25$

Range = 100.000

Mean = 82.120

Standard deviation = 21.363.

Note: Although the mean changes, adding a numerical value to each score does not change the average distance of each score from the mean. Therefore, the variance is not affected.

CALCULATOR EXPLORATION

Using the TI-73, TI-83, or TI-84 graphing calculator, you can easily calculate the mean and standard deviation by following these keystrokes.

TI-73

Step 1. Display list editor by pressing [LIST]. Under L1 enter all 25 scores from class A in Table 3.1.

```
L1      L2     L3      1
100     ------ ------
99
98
98
97
94
93
L1(1)=100
```

Step 2. Press 2nd [LIST] to activate STAT. Next, scroll to the right and select CALC. Next, scroll down to 1: 1 – Var Stats, press [1], then press ENTER.

```
Ls OPS MATH CALC
1:1-Var Stats
2:2-Var Stats
3:Manual-Fit
4:Med-Med
5:LinReg(ax+b)
6:QuadReg
7:ExpReg
```

```
1-Var Stats
x̄=77.12
Σx=1928
Σx²=159640
Sx=21.36258411
↓σx=20.93097227
n=25
```

TI-83/TI-84 Calculator
Step 1. First press [STAT]. Next, select 1: Edit by pressing 1. Here you can enter up to 999 elements. Under L1 enter all 25 scores from class A in Table 3.1.

```
L1      L2      L3      1
100    ------  ------
99
98
98
97
94
93
L1(1)=100
```

Step 2. Press [STAT] and scroll to CALC. Press 1: 1 – Var Stats.

```
EDIT CALC TESTS
1:1-Var Stats
2:2-Var Stats
3:Med-Med
4:LinReg(ax+b)
5:QuadReg
6:CubicReg
7↓QuartReg
```

Step 3. Press Enter to get your results.

```
1-Var Stats
 x̄=77.12
 Σx=1928
 Σx²=159640
 Sx=21.36258411
↓σx=20.93097227
■n=25
```

INTERNET RESOURCES

www.physics.csbsju.edu/stats/cstats_NROW_form.html

This section of the St. John's University website is a tool to calculate mean and standard deviation. After entering between 3 and 99 values, this program calculates mean and standard deviation. It also has an option that can import data from your computer, using copy and paste, and that can handle up to 1,024 numerical values.

www.edhelper.com/statistics.htm

This section of *edhelper.com* is a tutorial on mean and standard deviation. At the end of the tutorial, the website creates a practice worksheet and e-mails you the answers to the problems. This is an excellent resource for practicing your calculations.

www.statcan.ca/english/edu/power/ch12/variance.htm

This section of the website of Statistics Canada instructs users on the concept of standard deviation and variation. Also, this website provides links to the Canadian Census and other descriptive statistics that are compiled in Canada.

FURTHER READING

Allen, M. J. 2002. *Introduction to measurement theory.* Prospect Heights, IL: Waveland.

Christmann, E. P. 2002. Graphing calculators. *Science Scope* 2 (5): 46–48.

Christmann, E. P., and J. L. Badgett. 2001. A comparative analysis of the academic performances of elementary education preprofessionals, as disclosed by four methods of assessment. *Mid-Western Educational Researcher* 1 (2): 32–36.

Christmann, E. P., and J. L. Badgett. 1999. The comparative effectiveness of various microcomputer-based software packages on statistics achievement. *Computers in the Schools* 16 (1): 209–220.

Elmore, P. B., and P. L. Woehlke. 1997. *Basic statistics.* New York: Longman.

Gravetter, F. J., and L. B. Wallnau. 2002. *Essentials of statistics for the behavioral sciences.* New York: West.

Raymondu, J. C. 1999. *Statistical analysis in the behavioral sciences.* New York: McGraw Hill.

Thorne, B. M., and J. M. Giesen. 2000. *Statistics for the behavioral sciences.* Mountain View, CA: Mayfield Publishing.

Zawojewski, J. S., and J. M. Shaughnessy. 2000. Mean and median: Are they really so easy? *Mathematics Teaching in the Middle School* 5 (7): 436–440.

Chapter 4

STANDARD SCORES

OBJECTIVES

When you complete this chapter, you should be able to
1. demonstrate an understanding of percentile ranks and their relevance to classroom teachers;
2. compare the relationship between percentile ranks, standard scores, and the normal curve;
3. calculate percentile ranks from classroom and standardized test results;
4. find, use, and interpret measures of standard scores; and
5. compare and contrast T-scores, raw scores, and recentered test scores.

Key Terms

When you complete this chapter, you should be able to understand

centered score   standard score
percentile rank   T-score
raw score   z-score
relative standing

Standard scores show an individual's relative performance within a group. We are all familiar with standard scores and use them all the time: Your scores on the SAT are standard scores, as are individual scores on achievement tests, class rank, intelligence tests, and a variety of other aptitude tests. Standard scores will help you understand your students' standardized test results and explain the results to parents. Granted, you will view most of the results of your own classroom assessments as criterion-referenced data (number or percentage of items correct).

You must understand norm-referenced data (comparisons among local, state, and national scores), however, so that you can understand and then explain your students' and school's standardized test results. For example, if your school moves from the 10th to the 45th percentile as part of the Adequate Yearly Progress (AYP) mandated by the No Child Left Behind Act, you will

be able to explain your school's position in terms of its progress rather than having to rationalize why your school is below the 50th percentile. In addition, you would be able to justify your school's "inadequate" AYP if it ranks in the 95th percentile for two successive years.

In this chapter we will discuss the following types of standard scores: *percentile ranks, z-scores,* and *T-scores.* All are based on concepts—such as the mean, the normal distribution, and the standard deviation—already familiar to you from the last two chapters. In the case of class rank, however, keep in mind that a percentile rank from an ordinal scaled score or a rank score should be used. Z-scores, which are standard scores representing the number of standard deviation units a raw score is above or below the mean and which are used with normative data, are converted to percentile ranks when an individual score can be compared to a normal population (e.g., z-scores are calculated when the mean and the standard deviation from a population are known).

STANDARD SCORES IN SCHOOLS

Results on standardized tests are given as standard scores. On the SAT, the scores range from 200 to 800 with percentile ranks ranging from 1 to 99. Higher scores result from correctly answering more test questions. Both the score and the percentile rank compare the test taker's results with those of a recent representative national sample of high school students. A student's percentile rank shows the percentage of the test takers who earned scores at or below those of the student. For example, if a candidate's percentile rank is 70, the candidate's score is equal to that earned by 7 of 10 SAT test takers.

PERCENTILE RANKS

Percentile rank represents a student's position in a group relative to the number of students who scored at or below the position of that student. School districts use percentile ranks to calculate a student's rank within a class and to determine a student's relative standing on a standardized achievement or aptitude test. Test companies often report students' achievement test scores as percentile ranks. If a student scored at the 65th percentile on the reading test of the Stanford achievement tests, that student obtained scores as high as or higher than 65% of the students who took the test. To calculate percentile ranks, we use the concepts of the mean, standard deviation, and the normal distribution, as discussed in other chapters.

Class ranks are based on students' grade point averages, or GPAs. The first step in calculating percentile ranks, based on GPAs or any other score, is to arrange the scores in order from highest to lowest, as shown in Table 4.1. Data organized in this

Table 4.1

Grade Point Averages (GPAs) for a High School Senior Class

3.9798	3.537	2.7129	1.6813
3.9321	3.5203	2.6584	1.573
3.9147	3.5177	2.6346	1.54
3.8922	3.4266	2.5612	1.5259
3.881	3.4249	2.5272	1.5
3.8761	3.419	2.4242	1.4375
3.8755	3.4072	2.3673	1.4341
3.875	3.3314	2.3386	1.1324
3.8593	3.1734	2.3253	1.1226
3.8511	3.1492	2.2799	1.063
3.8457	3.1296	2.2409	0.9971
3.8358	3.0909	2.1742	0.9854
3.8295	3.0849	2.1275	0.9752
3.7991	3.0817	2.0535	0.8887
3.7926	3.0787	2.002	0.7889
3.7558	2.9518	1.9785	0.7771
3.6858	2.9485	1.9559	0.7456
3.6827	2.9479	1.949	0.6664
3.6752	2.9294	1.899	0.6558
3.6685	2.9229	1.8635	0.5555
3.646	2.8504	1.8366	0.4889
3.6305	2.8444	1.7358	0.488
3.63	2.7992	1.7347	0.4526
3.61	2.7481	1.7154	0.225
3.6023	2.7264	1.7008	0

Interpreting Assessment Data

way, from highest to lowest or lowest to highest, are referred to as *ordinal data*.

Once the data are organized in rank order (ordinally), a percentile rank (PR) can be calculated. Equation 4.1 is the formula used to calculate percentile rank (PR) from ordinal data. Percentile ranks are reported on a continuous 100-point scale.

Equation 4.1

$$PR = 100 - \frac{(100R - 50)}{N}$$

In Equation 4.1, "R" is the rank position and "N" is the sample size. Therefore, if we use Equation 4.1 to analyze the GPA data from Table 4.1, the student who ranked first in a class of 100 would be at the 99.5th percentile rank (see Calculation 4.1)

Calculation 4.1

$$PR = 100 - \frac{(100 * 1) - 50}{100} = 99.5\text{th PR}$$

Likewise, the student in the 50th rank position would be at the 50.5th percentile rank (see Calculation 4.2).

Calculation 4.2

$$PR = 100 - \frac{(100 * 50) - 50}{100} = 50.5\text{th PR}$$

Notice that the equation estimates the percentile rank as based at the midpoint of the interval, i.e., the midpoint of the interval (50 – 51) is 50.5. That means the percentile rank of the student in the 100th rank position would be the 0.5th percentile rank (see Calculation 4.3).

Calculation 4.3

$$PR = 100 - \frac{(100 * 100) - 50}{100} = 0.5\text{th PR}$$

Equation 4.1 is very useful for a guidance counselor who is interested in calculating the class rank of students within a particular senior class when a normal distribution is not available.

FRANCIS GALTON (1822–1911)

Francis Galton, Charles Darwin's cousin, became interested in measuring differences in the cognitive, affective, and psychomotor characteristics of people in England in the late 1800s. One of his studies reported measurements of the stature of 8,585 adult men. As reported by Galton, the mean height for men was 67.02 in., with a standard deviation of 2.564 in. Galton, being a statistician, plotted his findings as a frequency polygon, which showed that the results formed the shape of a normal curve (see Figure 4.1). As a result of Galton's research, scientists measure all sorts of other characteristics, such as weights, skull sizes, and reaction times.

Concurrent with Galton's research, an increasing number of students were attending *common schools* throughout the United States from the mid to late 1800s. Increased student attendance at common schools, which are known today as public schools, created a need for more teachers, resulting in the first teacher preparation institutions, called *normal schools*, opening their doors throughout the country.

We see that the similarities between the term *normal school* and the statistical term *normal distribution* are no coincidence when we consider that they evolved almost simultaneously with the norm-referenced testing theories of G. Stanley Hall, Charles Spearman, and E. L. Thorndike. As discussed in Chapter 2, normal distribution, which is also known as the *normal curve* or *bell curve*, refers to a distribution that is symmetrical: The areas on both sides of the curve are identical.

Moreover, school districts sometimes report progress on the basis of percentile ranks for scholarship eligibility and college admissions decisions.

NORMAL DISTRIBUTIONS AND PERCENTILES

To visualize a normal distribution, imagine being able to categorize each man on Earth along a parallel line according to height. Theoretically, if we were able to create stacks of their bodies according to their heights, we would see a mountain of men in the shape of a normal distribution (see Figure 4.1 for how this distribution would look). Keep in mind that, according to the Guinness Book of Word Records (2002), the tallest living man is 7 ft. 8.9 in., and the shortest man is 2 ft. 4 in. tall.

Recalling our discussion on central tendency, you will remember that when we are moving from left to right, the distribution is formed by a gradual movement upward from the extreme short height of 2 ft. 4 in. to the peak average height of about 5 ft. 7 in. Then the curve would gradually slope downward as the frequency of taller men diminished from the extreme height of 7 ft. 8.9 in. If we use Galton's statistics, the standard deviation for male height is about 2.56 in., with a mean height of 5 ft. 7 in., which is about the same as what we find in the United States today. Therefore, men who range in height between 5 ft. 4 in. and 5 ft. 10 in. are not considered unusual.

Applied to industry, most manufacturers of furniture, automobiles, beds, and other goods build consumer products within a range of 2 or 3 full standard deviations of human sizes, such as height, weight, and arm length. This is because, mathematically, three full standard deviations below and above the mean on a normal distribution are equivalent to about 99% of the normal curve area; or, in this case, 99% of the male population. This is mass production, or standardized production for a mass market.

More practical for the classroom teacher is being able to use percentile ranks and the normal distribution together to analyze a student's scores on different tests. The ability to interpret scores on standardized tests, such as the Wechsler Intelligence Scale for Children III (WISC III) and the SAT is essential. Moreover, being able to determine the percentile rank of an individual student from a *raw score*, the unadjusted score on a test, is a skill every teacher should have, because comparisons between IQ scores and standardized test results on the same scales will help you make relative comparisons between and among a variety of aptitude and achievement tests. For example, you can interpret the relative classroom performance of a youngster on the basis

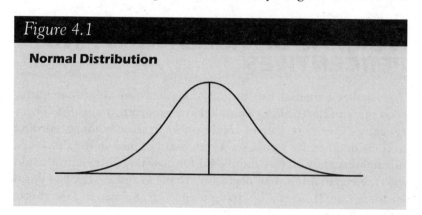

Figure 4.1

Normal Distribution

of a comparison among his or her results on an achievement test, grades, and, possibly, IQ test scores.

CHECK FOR UNDERSTANDING

4.1   From the data presented in Table 4.1, calculate the percentile rank (PR) of the student with a 3.6023 GPA.

4.2   What is the percentile rank of the student in the 73rd rank position?

4.3   Define percentile rank.

Z-SCORES AND PERCENTILE RANKS

A *standard score* is a score that shows the relative standing, or the exact location, of a raw score in a distribution. For example, a student's SAT score is a standard score, because it shows how well the student scored in relation to other students who took the SAT. A standard score can be computed if the mean and the standard deviation of a population distribution are known. If both are known and a very large population exists, the distribution will be very close to a perfectly symmetrical bell-shaped curve, which is also known as a normal curve or a normal distribution (see Chapter 2).

Although normal distributions are shaped alike and all are symmetrical, the scales for different tests are sometimes different. For example, the Wechsler IQ scale has a population mean (μ) = 100 and a population standard deviation (σ) = 15, while the Stanford-Binet IQ scale has a population mean (μ) = 100 and a population standard deviation (σ) = 16. Yet, even when the reported scales are slightly different, we can transform their data into standard deviation units by converting the scores into z-scores, which are standard scores representing the number of standard deviation units a raw score is above or below the mean. Equation 4.2 shows the formula for calculating a z-score.

Equation 4.2

$$z = \frac{x - \mu}{\sigma}$$

In equation 4.2, μ is the population mean, σ is the population standard deviation, and x is the raw score. The individual results of all norm-referenced standardized tests are based on a population mean and a population standard deviation; not the sample statistics that we discussed in previous chapters.

So what does a z-score tell us? The z-score tells us how many standard deviation units the raw score is above or below the mean (see Figure 4.3). Notice that a z-score of 0 is directly in the center of the normal distribution. A positive z-score of 1 is one standard deviation above the mean; a z-score of 2 is two standard deviations above the mean; a z-score of 3 is three standard deviations above the mean. Similarly, on the opposite side of the central point, a z-score of -1 is one standard deviation unit below the mean; a z-score of -2 is two standard deviation units below the mean; a z-score of -3 is three standard deviation units below the mean.

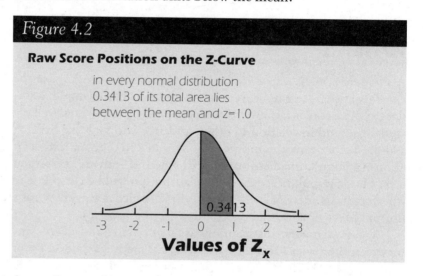

Figure 4.2

Raw Score Positions on the Z-Curve

in every normal distribution
0.3413 of its total area lies
between the mean and z=1.0

0.3413

-3   -2   -1   0   1   2   3

Values of Z$_x$

As our first application of z-scores, let's examine some results from the SAT. The Educational Testing Service (ETS) provides information on the interpretation of test results on its website at *http://professionals.collegeboard.com/gateway* for test administrations between 2001 and 2002 before the new, three-part SAT Reasoning Test was introduced. For the 1,276,320 test takers during that time span the population mean (μ) is 1020 for the combined verbal and mathematics sections, with a population standard deviation (σ) of 208 on the combined verbal and mathematics sections.

Knowing the mean and standard deviation, we are now able to calculate a z-score. If a student received a combined raw score of x = 1060 on the SAT, what would his or her z-score be? Calculation 4.4 computes a z-score using Equation 4.2.

Calculation 4.4

$$z = \frac{1060 - 1020}{208} = 0.192$$

Figure 4.3

Z-Scores and the Normal Distribution

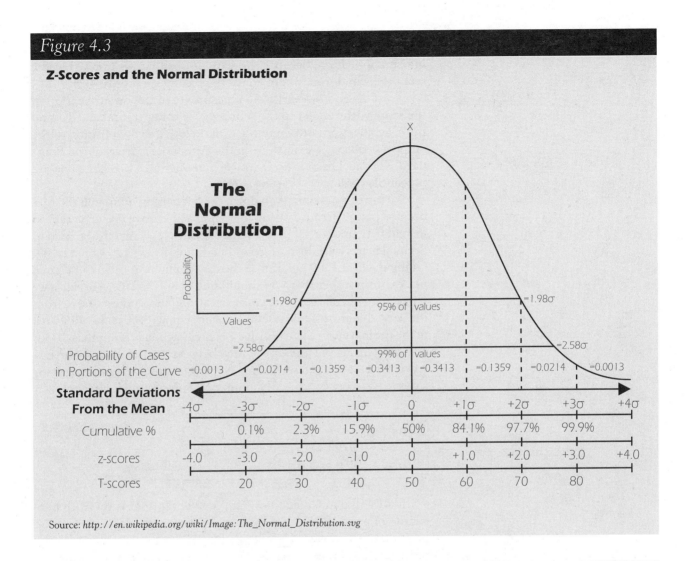

Source: http://en.wikipedia.org/wiki/Image:The_Normal_Distribution.svg

THE BIG TEST

Nicholas Lemann's *The Big Test* (2000) gives a history of the SAT and how it affected socioeconomic status in America. The book explains the SAT's impact on the construction of an American meritocracy, the system of reward based on merit. According to Lemann, James Bryant Conant and Henry Chauncey designed the SAT so that the brightest members of society, especially members of the underprivileged classes, could gain access to higher education. As a result, a new class of well-educated people emerged, and formerly disadvantaged groups entered the middle and upper socioeconomic levels of society. Lemann contends that, because of the SAT, America has shifted from an aristocracy-based social system to a merit-based social system. Ironically, however, many opponents of standardized testing argue that the SAT has become the gatekeeper for entry into the most prestigious colleges and universities in America. As a result, critics suggest that a high percentage of working class and minority students, who have traditionally not fared well on the SAT, have been denied upward social mobility because of low SAT scores.

The calculated z-score of 0.192 gives us some very important information. First, because the score is positive, we know that the score is located somewhere above the mean (see Figure 4.3).

This is, however, only an estimate of the exact location of the score with respect to the scores of the other test takers. To find the exact location, or percentile rank, relative to the position of the other test takers, we must go to the Appendix, Areas of the Standard Normal Distribution, which demonstrates how to calculate percentile rank.

To use this table, first go down the left column to match the first decimal place. Because we are matching a z-score of 0.192, you need to find 0.1, under "z" in the left column. Next, match the second decimal place with the corresponding numerical value, which is .09. Going down the .09 column to the row containing the first decimal places, the number that you should find is .0753. This is because we know that a normal curve is symmetrical, and the amount of area from the left tail to the middle point, or mean, equals 50% of the total area in the normal curve. The positive z-score that you just found is .0753, and this tells us the amount of area between the mean and our raw score. Calculation 4.5 shows how to calculate the percentile rank for a positive z-score by using the numerical value found in the table.

Calculation 4.5

0.5000 + 0.0753 = 0.5753
0.5753 * 100 = 57.53rd PR

Notice that in Calculation 4.5, 0.5000 represents the 50th percentile of area on the normal curve between the left tail and the position of the mean. The value of 0.0753 is the area between the mean and the exact location of the z-score. For example, when we add 0.5000 to 0.0753, we calculate a proportion of area that equals 0.5753 of the area within the normal curve. Moreover, to convert the proportion to a percentile rank, we must multiply the proportion by 100, which gives us a whole number. In this case, our z-score of 0.192 tells us that the SAT score of 1060 is at the 57.53rd percentile rank (PR). In other words, 57.53% of the test takers scored at or below the SAT raw score of 1060, which corresponds with the percentile rank data provided to test takers by ETS.

To determine the relative standing required for a student with an SAT raw score of 820, we can calculate a z-score and compute a percentile rank. The first step is to use Equation 4.2 to calculate the z-score. Calculation 4.6 shows the z-score calculation for an SAT score of 820.

> **Calculation 4.6**
>
> $$z = \frac{820 - 1020}{208} = -0.962$$

Remember, when calculating z-scores, you must know the population mean and standard deviation. Next, as in the previous z-score example in Calculation 4.5, we go to the Appendix, Areas of the Standard Normal Distribution, which will be used to compute a percentile rank. Again, take the value of the z-score, -0.96, and go down the left column to match the first decimal place, which is .09. By going across the row to .06, you should have found the numerical area proportion value of .3315 on the table. However, since the z-score is negative, you will need to subtract the proportion value from 0.500 rather than add. Calculation 4.7 shows how to calculate a percentile rank from a negative z-score by using the proportion value of 0.3315.

> **Calculation 4.7**
>
> $0.5000 - 0.3315 = 0.1685$
> $0.1685 * 100 = 16.85\text{th PR}$

Since a negative z-score is below the mean, we subtract the area difference between the position of the raw score and the mean. On the basis of our calculation, the SAT raw score of 820 is equivalent to a z-score of –0.96 and a relative standing at the 16.85th PR For those of you who may have taken the SAT before 1995, your scores have been recentered. Table 4.2 show how scores at the University of Virginia were recentered.

CHECK FOR UNDERSTANDING

4.4. Using Table 4.2, what is the recentered SAT total for a student who had an SAT total of 1220 in 1984?

4.5. If the population mean (μ) is 100 for the Stanford-Binet Intelligence Test, with a population standard deviation (σ) of 16, what are the z-score and percentile rank for a person who scored 110?

4.6. Calculate a Stanford-Binet raw score (x) from a z-score of –1.25, knowing that the population mean (μ) is 100, with a population standard deviation (σ) of 16.

Table 4.2

University of Virginia Recentered SAT Scores

Year	Non-recentered Scores			Recentered Scores[1]		
	SAT Verbal	SAT Math	SAT Total	SAT Verbal	SAT Math	SAT Total[2]
2007				645	662	1307
2006				654	671	1325
2005				653	667	1320
2004				659	671	1330
2003				654	670	1324
2002				647	668	1314
2001				648	665	1314
2000				643	661	1304
1999				648	659	1308
1998				646	658	1304
1997				643	656	1299
1996				643	653	1296
1995	576	651	1227	645	653	1298
1994	573	644	1217	642	647	1289
1993	572	643	1215	641	646	1287
1992	573	642	1215	642	645	1287
1991	573	641	1214	642	644	1286
1990	569	639	1208	638	642	1280

Year	Non-recentered Scores			Recentered Scores[1]		
	SAT Verbal	SAT Math	SAT Total	SAT Verbal	SAT Math	SAT Total
1989	577	641	1218	646	644	1290
1988	575	639	1214	645	642	1287
1987	585	645	1230	653	648	1301
1986	582	641	1223	650	644	1294
1985	586	635	1221	654	637	1291
1984	584	636	1220	652	638	1290
1983	579	623	1202	647	627	1274
1982	578	620	1198	647	625	1272
1981	567	607	1174	637	613	1250
1980	570	608	1178	639	613	1252
1979	584	615	1199	652	621	1273
1978	583	625	1208	652	629	1281
1977	588	620	1208	656	624	1280

[1] In April 1995, Educational Testing Service began recentering SAT scores so that the national mean scores for verbal and math would both be very close to 500. This caused mean verbal scores at UVa to increase by approximately 70 points, but had little impact on mean math scores at UVa. Although recentered scores did not exist for classes that entered before 1996, they have been calculated and reported above so scores for the years 1995 and earlier can be compared to the recentered scores.

[2] In some cases the mean recentered SAT total score does not equal the sum of the mean verbal plus the mean math score because the verbal and math means have been rounded to the nearest integer.

Note: Figures do not include transfer students.

Source: www.web.virginia.edu/iaas/data_catalog/institutional/data_digest/adm_total.htm

Z-SCORES, PERCENTILE RANK, AND IQ SCORES

Because public school teachers work with a variety of students who span a spectrum of cognitive abilities, it is important to discuss relative standing as it relates to intelligence quotient (IQ) scores. Table 4.3 shows the range of IQ classifications, displaying ranges from 65 and below to 128 and above. In general, teachers should understand that a typical class of students is composed of students who range in reported IQ from about 85 to 130, according to the Wechsler IQ Scale. In this case, what percentage of students from a normal population does this include? The first step to solve this problem is to calculate the z-score for a raw score of 85 (see Calculation 4.8). Next, calculate a z-score for a raw score of 130 (see Calculation 4.9).

Calculation 4.8

$$z = \frac{85 - 100}{15} = -1.00$$

Calculation 4.9

$$z = \frac{130 - 100}{15} = 2.00$$

After calculating a z-score of –1.00 for a raw IQ score of 85, along with the z-score of 2.00 for an IQ score of 130, we must then compute an area interval to determine the percentage of students falling within this range (See Figure 4.3). To do this, we must first find the area from the z-score of –1.00 to the center of the normal distribution, where the z-score is 0.00 (The z-score of 0 is in the same position as the mean). You can see the numerical area proportion associated with the interval value of 0.3413 in the Appendix, Areas of the Standard Normal Distribution.

Next, we need to find the area from the z-score of 2.00 to the center of the normal distribution, where the z-score is 0.00. (Again, the z-score of 0 is in the same position as the mean.) This is also seen as the numerical area proportion associated with the interval value of 0.4772 in the Appendix, Areas of the Standard Normal Distribution.

Now that we have calculated the area intervals, we need to add them together to compute the total area. Calculation 4.10 shows how to calculate an area interval proportion into a percentage.

Interpreting Assessment Data

<table>
<tr><td colspan="2">Calculation 4.10</td></tr>
<tr><td>0.3413 + 0.4772 = 0.8185
0.8185 * 100 = 81.85%</td></tr>
</table>

0.3413 + 0.4772 = 0.8185

0.8185 * 100 = 81.85%

Calculation 4.10

We know that 81.85% of the population have IQ ranges between 85 and 130. Undoubtedly, this teaching dynamic creates a complicated state of affairs for the classroom teacher, given that the students in a typical classroom can range in abilities from "dull normal" to "very superior" (See Table 4.3). Moreover, this statistic also shows us that special educators, for the most part, work with about 18.15% of the student population, assuming that special education participation is based on cognitive abilities (some children have vision problems, hearing problems, or other problems, which often are unrelated to cognitive abilities).

Table 4.3

IQ Classifications and Percentile Rank

Classification	IQ Limits	Percent Included
Very Superior	128 and over	2.2
Superior	120–127	6.7
Bright Normal	111–119	16.1
Average	91–110	50
Dull Normal	80–90	16.1
Borderline	66–79	6.7
Defective	65 and below	2.2

INTERPRETING ITBS SCORES

A *raw score* is the number of items that a student answers correctly on a test. For example, if Justin's raw score is 7 on the mathematics section of the Iowa Test of Basic Skills (ITBS) test and his raw score is 10 on the science section of the ITBS, we cannot conclude that his achievement is the same in mathematics and science. Therefore, raw scores are usually converted to standard scores (SS) or percentile ranks (PR).

A *standard score* (SS) is a numerical value that locates a student's academic achievement on a standard scale. With the ITBS, standard scores are based on the median performance of students during the spring of each academic year. Therefore, a score of 150 for a first-grade student indicates that this student is at the median level for all first graders who took this test. A standard score of 150 is the median performance of students in the spring of grade one. For eighth graders, the median performance in the spring is a standard score of 250.

Grade	1	2	3	4	5	6	7	8
SS	150	168	185	200	214	227	239	250

With the ITBS, a student's percentile rank can vary, depending on which group is used to determine the ranking. For example, a student is simultaneously a member of many different groups—among them being all students in his or her classroom, building, school district, state, and the nation. Different sets of percentile ranks permit schools to make the most relevant comparisons involving their students.

CHECK FOR UNDERSTANDING

4.7. Based on the IQ classifications in Table 4.3, how would a child with an IQ of 110 be classified?

4.8. Compute a z-score and percentile rank for a student who has an IQ of 97. Assume that we are using the Wechsler scale, what is this student's IQ classification according to Table 4.3?

4.9. What percentage of students have IQ scores over 130 on the Wechsler Scale. What would students with IQs exceeding 130 be classified as according to Table 4.3?

T-SCORES

A *T-score* is an alternative to the z-score that uses a mean of 50 as its central point, with a standard deviation of 10. All z-scores can be converted to T-scores. The formula for converting a z-score to a T-score is found in Equation 4.3. A T-score converts a z-score to a 100-point scale. This system is preferable because T-scores produce only positive integers, whereas z-scores can be reported as negative. For example if a boy's standardized test score is reported as z = -0.50, the T-score equivalent is 45.

Equation 4.3

$$T = 50 + (10 * z\text{-score})$$

As an example, the T-score that is equivalent to a z-score of 2.2 is computed in Calculation 4.11.

Calculation 4.11

$$T\text{-score} = 50 + (10 * 2.20) = 72$$

Figure 4.3 shows the relationships among z-scores and T-scores. Notice that each scale has a common feature in that the original scores can be located in relation to the mean and standard deviation unit. One advantage of working with T-scores is that all scores can be put on a standard scale without the confusion of having to work with negative or obscure numbers.

CHECK FOR UNDERSTANDING

4.10.   What T-score is equivalent to a z-score of -1.50?

4.11.   What T-score is equivalent to an SAT score of 1050?

4.12.   Knowing that a T-score is 40, calculate the corresponding z-score.

CHALLENGE QUESTION

4.13.   Given a normal distribution with a population mean of 100 and a standard deviation of 15, find the percentile ranks for the following raw scores.
a. 145
b. 130
c. 115

d. 100

e. 85

f. 70

IN SUMMARY

A *percentile rank* is the percentage of students whose scores fall at or below a particular score. Percentile ranks are computed by calculating a standard score called a z-score, which can be used to translate an individual's performance within a group. Percentile ranks are used by teachers to report a student's relative position among a group of students in terms of those students who are at or below that student's level of achievement or aptitude. Standardized tests, such as the SAT, Wechsler IQ Test, and the Iowa Tests of Basic Skills (ITBS), are reported as norm-referenced population data. Therefore, scores from these tests can be converted into standard scores, such as z-scores and T-scores, and can be used to compute a student's relative standing as percentile rank. Teachers can use relative standing to report progress and gauge the effectiveness of their own teaching.

CALCULATOR EXPLORATION

Using the TI-83 or TI-84 graphing calculator, you can easily compute the percentage of students by area by following these key strokes.

Problem: Determine the percentage of students in a normal distribution who fall between an IQ range of 85 and 130. Since an 85 IQ is 1 standard deviation unit below the mean (equivalent to a z-score of –1.00) and an IQ of 130 is 2 standard deviation units above the mean (equivalent to a z-score of 2.00), we will use the TI-83 graphing calculator to determine the percentage of students in a normal distribution who fall within this range of scores.

TI-83/TI-84

Step 1. First press 2nd VARS, to activate the distribution function. Next, select 2: normalcdf (by pressing 2).

Step 2. Next, enter the corresponding lower z-score of –1, insert a comma, and enter the higher z-score of +2 and close the parenthesis. Next press ENTER.

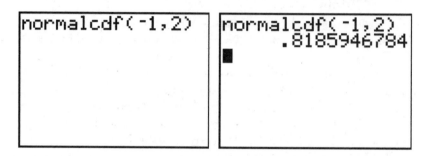

Note: The calculator has computed the proportion of area in a normal curve that corresponds with this range of scores. To get the percentage, you should multiply the proportion by 100. Thus, by going out four decimal places, (0.8185 * 100 = 81.85%), which is a much easier way to determine the area than the table that we used earlier in the chapter.

CHAPTER REVIEW QUESTIONS

4.14.   Of the following z-scores, which value indicates the greatest numerical distance from the mean?
   a. z = -1.00
   b. z = +1.75
   c. z = -2.75
   d. z = +2.50

4.15.   If the Wechsler IQ scale has a population mean (μ) = 100 and a population standard deviation (σ) = 15, what is the z-score for a student scoring 80 on the Wechsler IQ test?

4.16.   Based on the z-score calculated in question 4.14, what is the percentile rank of a student who scores 80 on the Wechsler IQ test?

4.17.   If the Wechsler IQ scale has a population mean (μ) = 100 and a population standard deviation (σ) = 15, what is the z-score for a student scoring 120 on the Wechsler IQ test?

4.18.   Based on the z-score calculated in question 4.16, what is the percentile rank of a student who scores 120 on the Wechsler IQ test?

4.19.   If the Stanford-Binet IQ scale has a population mean (μ) = 100 and a population standard deviation (σ) = 16, what is the z-score for a student scoring 80 on the Stanford-Binet IQ test?

4.20. Based on the z-score calculated in question 4.19, what is the percentile rank of a student who scores 80 on the Stanford-Binet IQ test?

4.21. If the Stanford-Binet IQ scale has a population mean (μ) = 100 and a population standard deviation (σ) = 16, what is the z-score for a student scoring 120 on the Stanford-Binet IQ test?

4.22. Based on the z-score calculated in question 4.21, what is the percentile rank of a student who scores 120 on the Stanford-Binet IQ test?

4.23. The population mean (μ) is 1020 for the combined verbal and mathematics sections of the SAT, with a population standard deviation (σ) of 208 on the combined verbal and mathematics sections. Calculate the following:

a. A z-score for a combined SAT score of 1270.
b. A percentile rank for a combined SAT score of 1270.
c. A T-score for for a combined SAT score of 1270.
d. A z-score for a combined SAT score of 770.
e. A percentile rank for a combined SAT score of 770.
f. A T-score for for a combined SAT score of 770.

4.24. Explain the meaning of percentile ranks and recentered scores.

ANSWERS: CHECK FOR UNDERSTANDING

4.1. 75.5th percentile rank

4.2. 27.5th percentile rank

4.3. A percentile rank is the percentage of scores that falls below a given score. Sometimes the percentage is defined to include all scores that fall at the point; sometimes the percentage is defined to include half of the scores at the point.

4.4. 1290

4.5. z-score = 0.625, percentile rank = 73.57th PR

4.6. The subject would have an IQ raw score of 80.

4.7. This student is classified as average.

4.8. The z-score is -0.20, with a relative standing at the 42.07th PR. This student is classified as average, according to Table 4.3.

4.9. 2.28% of all students. All students with IQs above 130 fall into Table 4.3's "very superior" classification.

4.10. T-score is 35.

4.11. T-score is 51.44.

4.12. z-score equals -1.00.

ANSWER: CHALLENGE QUESTION

4.13.   a. 145 = 99.87th PR
      b. 130 = 97.72nd PR
      c. 115 = 84.13rd PR
      d. 100 = 50th PR
      e. 85 = 15.87th PR
      f. 70 = 2.28th PR

ANSWERS: CHAPTER REVIEW QUESTIONS

4.14.   c. $z = -2.75$
4.15. $z = -1.33$
4.16.   PR = 9.18th
4.17. $z = +1.33$
4.18.   PR = 90.82nd
4.19. $z = -1.25$
4.20.   PR = 10.56th
4.21. $z = -1.25$
4.22.   PR = 89.44th
4.23.   a. $z = 1.20$
      b. 88.49th PR
      c. $T = 62$
      d. $z = -1.20$
      e. 11.51st PR
      f. $T = 36.80$

4.24.   Percentile ranks are the relative standing of a score in a distribution of scores. The percentile rank is the relative standing at or below the raw score. Recentering of scores occurs when variables such as the mean and standard deviation are changed. For example, in April 1995, Educational Testing Service began recentering SAT scores so that the national mean scores for verbal and math would both be very close to 500.

INTERNET RESOURCES

www.teachersandfamilies.com/open/parent/scores2.cfm
    This part of the Teachers and Families website gives a general overview of percentiles and standard scores. The site is designed for someone who has a minimal understanding of the interpretation of test scores. It is a useful resource for practicing teachers to use as a reference, as well as a good site to suggest to parents who have test interpretation questions.

www.education.uiowa.edu/itp/itbs/itbs_interp_score.htm
    Because the Iowa Tests of Basic Skills (ITBS) is used throughout

the nation from grades K through 8, this site can be used by elementary and middle school teachers as a model depicting an essential standardized achievement test.

http://psych.colorado.edu/~mcclella/java/normal/normz.html
This site, by Professor Gary McClelland of the University of Colorado, offers a z-score calculator and the corresponding probabilities, which are equivalent to area calculations. This is a handy resource for students looking for additional information about z-scores.

REFERENCES

Lemann, N. 2000. *The big test: The secret history of the American meritocracy.* New York: Farrar, Straus, and Giroux.

FURTHER READING

American Educational Research Association (AERA). 1999. *Standards for educational and psychological testing.* Washington, DC: American Educational Research Association.

Brown, J. R. 1991. The retrograde motion of planets and children: Interpreting percentile rank. *Psychology in the Schools* 28 (4): 345–353.

Journal of School Improvement. 2000. What is this standard score stuff, anyway? *Journal of School Improvement* 1 (2): 44–45.

Pearson, K. 1930. *Life, letters, and labours of Francis Galton.* Vol. IIIa, correlation, personal identification, and eugenics. Cambridge, England: Cambridge University Press.

Raymondu, J. C. 1999. *Statistical analysis in the behavioral sciences.* New York: McGraw Hill.

Thorne, B. M., and J. M. Giesen, 2000. *Statistics for the behavioral sciences.* Mountain View, CA: Mayfield.

Zawojewski, J. S., and J. M. Shaughnessy. 2000. Mean and median: Are they really so easy? *Mathematics Teaching in the Middle School* 5 (7): 436–440.

Chapter 5

CORRELATION

OBJECTIVES

When you complete this chapter, you should be able to
1. recognize the strength and type of relationship between two variables,
2. demonstrate an understanding of a correlation coefficient,
3. select and use appropriate statistical methods to compute a correlation coefficient,
4. read and interpret a scatter plot, and
5. compute Pearson and Spearman rank-order correlation coefficients.

Key Terms

When you complete this chapter, you should be able to understand
    correlation coefficient
    Pearson correlation coefficient
    relationship
    scatter plot
    Spearman rank-order correlation coefficient

Thus far, we have explored individual statistics, which illustrate individual sets of scores through frequencies, central tendency, and variance. Sometimes, however, you will find it necessary to determine the relationship between two sets of scores. For example, are high SAT verbal scores (now called critical reading scores) associated with high college English grades? Do high-ability students tend to excel in all of their academic subjects? This chapter will discuss the concept of *correlation*, which is used in later chapters that will explain the concepts of validity and reliability. Here, we introduce the Pearson correlation coefficient, a statistic that is used with ratio or interval-scaled data. In addition, we introduce the Spearman correlation, which is used with ranked or ordinal-scaled data.

THE PEARSON CORRELATION COEFFICIENT

The *correlation coefficient* is a statistic that illustrates the existence of a linear relationship between two variables. It also expresses the strength of the relationship. For example, you might ask the question, are higher teacher salaries linked to higher academic achievement scores among students in a school district?

The numerical values of a correlation coefficient range between –1.00 and +1.00. The higher the numerical value, the stronger the relationship between the two variables (see Table 5.1). If the coefficient has a positive sign, the relationship is positive: If one value is high, the other value is high. Conversely, if the coefficient is negative, the relationship is negative: If one value is high, the other value is low.

For example, when a correlation coefficient is positive, if x is high, so is y. You would expect that a person who scores high on an algebra aptitude test would also obtain high grades in algebra. The correlation is also positive when a low value for x corresponds to a low value for y.

Conversely, if a correlation is negative, high scores on x are associated with low scores on y.

As an example, let's look at the relationship between the SAT math scores and the trigonometry grades of 10th, 11th, and 12th graders. Table 5.2 shows these students' SAT mathematics scores and trigonometry grades. To determine the correlation coefficient, we will calculate the Pearson for this set of scores.

Table 5.1

Interpretations of Correlations

Correlation	Interpretation
0.000 to 0.200	Very Weak
0.201 to 0.400	Weak
0.401 to 0.600	Moderate
0.601 to 0.800	Strong
0.801 to 1.000	Very Strong

Note: Numerical values can be plus or minus.

Table 5.2

SAT Math Scores and Trigonometry Achievement Scores

Forrest	740	95
Jamal	680	90
Alexandra	660	90
Lauren	550	86
Sabrina	500	80
Roberto	480	80
Chang	500	75
Jane	470	75
Rick	480	70
Pete	400	65

The *Pearson correlation coefficient*, sometimes called the *Pearson product-moment correlation*, is a measure of the linear relationship between the paired values of two variables (x and y). The equation takes into account each paired value and uses the mean, standard deviation, and z-score formulas in its computation (see Equation 5.1).

$$r = \frac{\sum (x - \overline{x})(y - \overline{y})}{(n-1)\, S_x S_y}$$

Equation 5.1

In this equation, $(x - \overline{x})$ is the deviation of the x variable from the mean, $(y - \overline{y})$ is the deviation of the y variable from the mean, S_x is the sample standard deviation for the x variable, S_y is the sample standard deviation for the y variable, and n represents the number of pairs of scores. To simplify this equation, we will represent r as the average value of the products of paired z-scores. This formula is found in Equation 5.2.

$$r = \frac{\sum z_x z_y}{n-1}$$

Equation 5.2

As our first example, we will examine the relationship between SAT mathematics scores and the percentage scores from a 12th-grade trigonometry class. Table 5.1 shows the relationship between the two variables, using the definitional formula given in Equation 5.2.

Table 5.3

Pearson Correlation Calculation

Student	SAT (x)	Trig. Grade (y)	$z_x = (x - \overline{x})/S_x$	$z_y = (y - \overline{y})/S_y$	$z_x z_y$
Forrest	740	95	1.77	1.50	2.66
Jamal	680	90	1.22	0.98	1.20
Alexandra	660	90	1.04	0.98	1.02
Lauren	550	86	0.04	-0.57	0.02
Sabrina	500	80	-0.42	-0.05	0.02
Rob	480	80	-0.60	-0.05	0.03
Chang	500	75	-0.42	-0.57	0.24
Jane	470	75	-0.69	-0.67	0.46
Rick	480	70	-0.60	-1.08	0.65
Pete	400	65	-1.33	-1.60	2.13
	$\overline{x} = 546$ $S_x = 109.87$	$\overline{y} = 80.50$ $S_y = 9.69$			$\sum z_x z_y = 8.43$

Interpreting Assessment Data

Notice that, for each variable (x and y), z-scores are calculated to transform the data onto the same scale. Next z_x is multiplied by z_y and then summed with the formula $\Sigma z_x z_y$, which will total to a positive sum value when a majority of positive z_x scores is multiplied by positive z_y scores, or, in a negative sum value, when a majority of positive z_x scores is multiplied by negative z_y scores. Calculation 5.1 shows that $r = 0.94$, which translates to a very strong positive correlation between SAT math scores and trigonometry scores. Therefore, we can conclude that high SAT scores are positively related to high trigonometry scores.

$$r = \frac{\sum z_x z_y}{n - 1}$$

or

$$r = \frac{8.43}{10 - 1} = 0.94$$

Calculation 5.1

CALCULATOR EXPLORATION

Using either the TI-73, TI-83, or TI-84 graphing calculator, you can easily compute a correlation coefficient by following these keystrokes.

TI-73

Step 1. Display list editor by pressing LIST. Here, you can enter up to 999 elements. Under L1, list all of the scores from the SATs that are listed in Table 5.3. Next, under L2, list all of the scores listed under trigonometry grades in Table 5.3.

L1	L2	L3	2
740	95	------	
680	90		
660	90		
550	86		
500	80		
480	80		
500	75		

L2(1) =95

Step 2. Press 2nd LIST to activate STAT. Next, scroll to the right and select CALC. Next, scroll down to 5: LinReg (ax+b), press 5, then press ENTER.

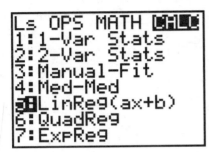

Step 3. Press 2nd APPS to activate VARS. Next, scroll down to 3: Statistics, and press 3. Next, scroll over to EQ and scroll down to 5: r, select 5, and press ENTER. Press ENTER again to get the correlation coefficient.

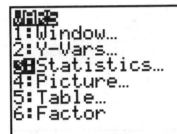 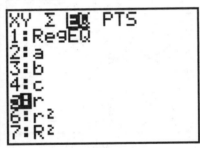

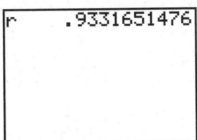

TI-83/TI-84

Step 1. First press STAT. Next, select 1: Edit by pressing 1. Here you can enter up to 999 elements. Under L1, list all of the scores from the SATs that are listed in Table 5.3. Next, under L2, list all of the scores listed under trigonometry grades in Table 5.3.

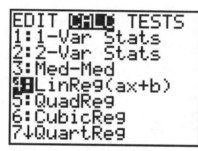

Step 2. Press STAT and scroll to the right and select CALC. Next, scroll down to 4: LinReg (ax+b), press 4, and press ENTER.

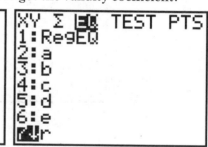

Step 3. Press VARS. Next, scroll down to 5: Statistics and press 5. Next, scroll over to EQ. Next, scroll down to 7: r and press 7. Press ENTER again to get the validity coefficient.

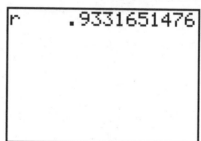

Correlation and Cause and Effect

People often think that correlation means the same thing as causation. Although a correlation means there is a relationship between two variables, it does not mean that one causes the other. For example, there is a positive correlation between ice cream consumption and death by drowning. However, common sense tells us that eating ice cream does not cause death by drowning; simply, when the weather is hot, more people eat ice cream and more people go swimming! As a further example, a plot of monthly sales of ice cream against monthly deaths from heart disease would show a negative correlation. Again, based on hundreds of research studies, it is hardly likely that eating ice cream protects from heart disease. It is simply that the mortality rate from heart disease is inversely related—and ice cream consumption positively related—to a third factor: environmental temperature. It is important to understand that a high correlation between two variables does not imply that one causes the other.

SCATTER PLOTS

The relationship between two variables can be illustrated in a *scatter plot,* which is a graph showing the paired scores. Figure 5.1 shows a scatter plot for SAT mathematics section scores and trigonometry grades. Notice that, because our relationship is very close to a perfect +1.0, it is almost a straight line.

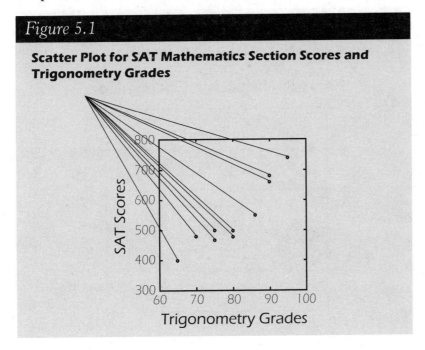

Figure 5.1

Scatter Plot for SAT Mathematics Section Scores and Trigonometry Grades

Figure 5.2 is a scatter plot of a perfect +1.00 correlation. In this case, we have positive scores for variables *x* and *y*. Likewise, since variable *x* is Fahrenheit temperature and variable *y* is the corresponding centigrade temperature, this scatter plot shows a perfectly straight line, which is known as a regression line.

Figure 5.2

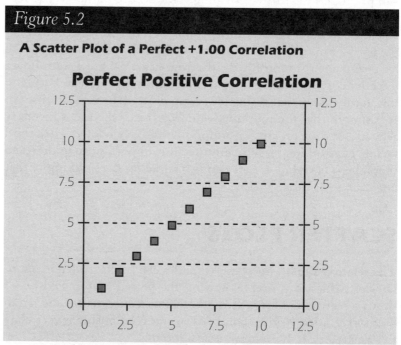

A Scatter Plot of a Perfect +1.00 Correlation

Figure 5.3

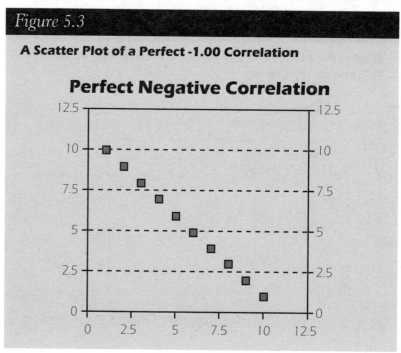

A Scatter Plot of a Perfect -1.00 Correlation

Figure 5.3 shows a scatter plot of a perfect -1.00 correlation. It shows the average velocity (*x*) to the race time (*y*) of a person running a 5k race, we would find that as the runner's running speed increases, his or her time decreases, giving us a perfect negative correlation.

Figure 5.4 shows a scatter plot of a high positive correlation between people's heights (*x*) and weights (*y*).

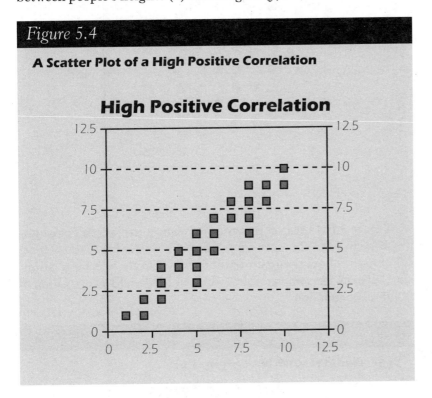

Figure 5.4

A Scatter Plot of a High Positive Correlation

High Positive Correlation

Figure 5.5 shows a scatter plot of a low negative correlation. The scatter plot compares the amount of money spent on education (*x*) with test scores (*y*), showing that as spending increases slightly, academic achievement slightly decreases, giving us a low negative correlation between the two variables (Christmann and Badgett 2000). It is important to remember, however, that a correlation shows only that two variables are related; it does not show a cause and effect relationship. This happens because slight increases in teachers' pay do not affect how hard teachers work—which would often result in higher academic achievement. In essence, most teachers are dedicated professionals who put forth great effort regardless of pay increases.

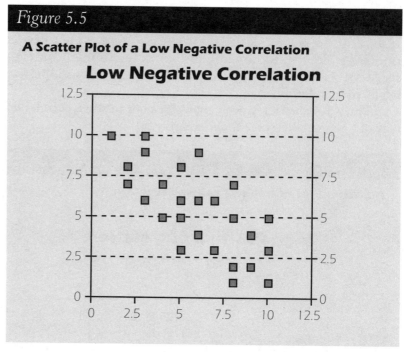

Figure 5.5

A Scatter Plot of a Low Negative Correlation

Figure 5.6 is a scatter plot that shows no correlation. For example, if we were to compare combined SAT scores (x) to the heights (y) of high school seniors, we would find that there is no relationship between the two variables, which should yield a correlation of 0, for no correlation.

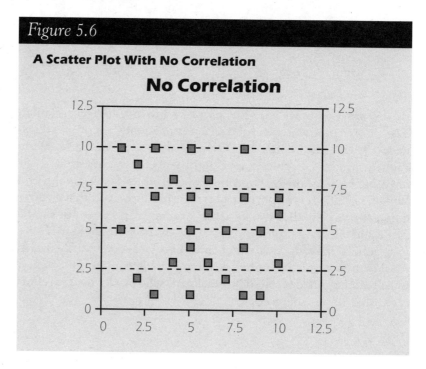

Figure 5.6

A Scatter Plot With No Correlation

CHECK FOR UNDERSTANDING

5.1.   Which correlation coefficient shows the weakest relationship?
a. + 0.94
b. - 0.77
c. + 0.15
d. - 0.22

5.2.   Calculate a Pearson correlation coefficient between the two variables given in the table to the right.

5.3.   How would the calculated correlation coefficient from question 5.2 be classified according to the categories given in Table 5.1?

(x)	(y)
100	77
95	76
90	80
85	70
80	75
75	74
70	72
65	75
60	69
55	60

5.4.   How would you best describe the scatter plot below?
a. A scatter plot with no correlation
b. A perfect positive correlation
c. A low negative correlation
d. A high positive correlation

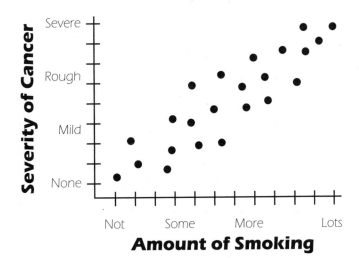

SPEARMAN RANK-ORDER CORRELATION COEFFICIENT

The *Spearman rank-order correlation coefficient* describes the linear relationship between two variables that are ranked on an ordinal scale of measurement. For example, you could use the Spearman rank-order coefficient to show such things as academic achievement based on class rank and IQ.

The symbol r_s represents the Spearman correlation coefficient (see Equation 5.3). Just like the Pearson r correlation coefficient, the Spearman correlation ranges between -1.00 and +1.00. We interpret the strength of a Spearman rank-order correlation the same way we interpret the strength of the correlations in Table 5.1.

$$r_s = 1 - \frac{6\Sigma D^2}{n(n^2 - 1)}$$

Equation 5.3

For example, suppose we are interested in whether 12th-grade students' GPAs are related to their rankings on the SAT (see Table 5.4). The first step in calculating a Spearman rank-order correlation, as shown in Table 5.4, is to rank the GPAs and the SAT scores. Once the scores have been ranked, we subtract the difference between the ranks, D. Next we square the differences (D^2) and compute the sum of the squared differences, ΣD^2. Then, as illustrated in Equation 5.3, we use the Spearman formula to determine a correlation coefficient:

r_s = The Spearman rank-order correlation coefficient,
D = The difference between the ranks on the two variables,
n = The number of individuals or pairs of ranks.

Calculation 5.3 shows how to use the formula to obtain a Spearman rank-order correlation coefficient.

Table 5.4

Twelfth Graders' GPAs and Combined SAT Scores

Student	GPA	Rank	SAT	Rank	D	D²
John Henry	3.97	1	1180	3	-1	1
Kate	3.85	2.5*	1130	6	-3.50	12.25
Wyatt	3.85	2.5*	1070	8	-5.50	30.25
Mattie	3.67	4	1180	3	1	1
Virgil	3.52	5	1140	5	0	0
Johnny	3.42	6	1090	1	5	25
Josephine	3.36	7	960	9	-2	4
Billy	3.24	8	1180	3	5	25
Jack	2.74	9	1110	7	2	4
Ike	2.56	10	720	10	0	0
						$\Sigma D^2 =$ 102.50

When ties occur on x or y, assign the average of the rank involved to each score, e.g., $\frac{2+3}{2} = 2.50$.

Calculation 5.2

$$r_s = 1 - \frac{6\Sigma (D^2)}{n(n^2 - 1)}$$

Step 1

$$r_s = 1 - \frac{6\Sigma (102.5)}{10(10^2 - 1)}$$

Step 2

$$r_s = 1 - \frac{615}{990}$$

Step 3

$$r_s = 1 - 0.621 = 0.379$$

Calculation 5.2 shows that $r_s = 0.379$, which is interpreted as a weak positive relationship between GPA and combined SAT scores. Therefore, the example shows that GPA is not a very good predictor of SAT scores and that other predictors, such as motivaton and achievement test results, should be considered.

CHECK FOR UNDERSTANDING

5.5.   Which scale of measurement is required for a Spearman rank-order correlation?
a. Ratio
b. Interval
c. Ordinal
d. Nominal

5.6.   Find the Spearman rank-order correlation coefficient between the two sets of scores.

	Scores	
Student	Reading	IQ
A	98	145
B	91	135
C	88	125
D	85	120
E	80	110
F	75	105
G	70	95
H	74	95
I	65	90
J	60	80

5.7.   Based on your calculated Spearman correlation coefficient from question 5.6, explain the strength of the relationship between reading scores and IQ scores (very weak, moderate, or strong, for instance) and determine the direction of the relationship (is it positive or negative)?

IN SUMMARY

The correlation coefficient helps us understand the relationship between two variables. The Pearson product-moment correlation, the most commonly used correlation statistic, is used with either an interval or a ratio scale of measurement. The Spearman rank-order correlation examines the relationship between two variables that are on an ordinal scale.

All coefficients of correlation range from -1.0 to +1.0, with the direction of the relationship shown by the sign (+ or -), and the strength of the relationship is based on its numerical value. For example, a correlation coefficient of zero indicates that there is no correlation between two variables, whereas a positive correlation shows that as the numerical values associated with one variable increase, the numerical values associated with the other variable increase as well. With a negative correlation, as one variable increases, the other variable decreases. A correlation statistic only shows the relative strength of a linear relationship between two variables. It does not imply a cause-and-effect relationship between two variables.

Classroom teachers use correlation to explore relationships between variables. For example, is intelligence related to academic achievement? The next two chapters cover validity and reliability, which deal with the concept of correlation. Therefore, to answer questions related to validity and reliability, an understanding of correlation is necessary.

CHAPTER REVIEW QUESTIONS

5.8. How is a Pearson correlation coefficient different from a Spearman correlation?

5.9. Explain how to calculate a Pearson correlation coefficient.

5.10. The numerical value for a correlation ranges between
a. 0.00 and +1.00.
b. –1.00 and 0.00.
c. –1.00 and +1.00.
d. none of the above.

5.11. What does the Pearson correlation coefficient measure?

5.12. A scatter plot shows a data set spread in a circular pattern. Which correlation coefficient would best describe the correlation for these data?
a. 0.00
b. 1.00
c. -.50
d. all of the above

5.13. For a Pearson correlation coefficient of –1.90 between test X and test Y, the correlation indicates that
a. as scores on test X increase, scores on test Y decrease.
b. as scores on test X increase, scores on test Y increase.
c. as scores on test X decrease, scores on test Y decrease.
d. none of the above.

5.14. Calculate a Pearson correlation coefficient for the following sets of test scores.

Student	Test A	Test B
A	98	100
B	71	81
C	85	66
D	64	50

5.15. If the original data are measured on an ordinal scale of measurement, what type of correlation should you use?
a. Pearson
b. Spearman
c. Gaussian
d. all of the above

5.16. Calculate a Spearman correlation for the following sets of ranked test scores.

Student	SAT (combined)	GPA
A	1420	3.90
B	1100	3.00
C	1050	2.80
D	980	3.00
E	700	1.68

5.17. A researcher finds a high positive correlation between price of school lunches and achievement test scores. As a result, the researcher concludes that more expensive lunches cause test scores to increase. Do you agree or disagree with the researcher's conclusion? Please explain your decision.

ANSWERS: CHECK FOR UNDERSTANDING

5.1. c. + 0.15
5.2. + 0.733
5.3. A strong positive correlation
5.4. d. A high positive correlation
5.5. e. Ordinal
5.6. $r_s = 0.997$
5.7. There is a very strong positive correlation. This means as one score increases the other increases.

ANSWERS: CHAPTER REVIEW QUESTIONS

5.8. The Pearson and Spearman coefficients are mathematically identical. However, the Spearman rank coefficient is calculated from the ranks of each variable, not the actual values.

5.9. The Pearson correlation coefficient is calculated based on the following formula that uses your z-scores:

$$r = \frac{\sum z_x z_y}{n-1}$$

5.10. c. -1.00 and 1.00.

5.11. The purpose of the Pearson correlation coefficient is to indicate a linear relationship between two measurement variables. This means that if you have two sets of scores, you can determine if one score predicts another score.

5.12. a. 0.00

5.13. d. None of the above

5.14. Correlation coefficient (r) = 0.7752

5.15. b. Spearman

5.16. Spearman r = 0.825 (corrected for ties)

5.17. Because correlation does not establish cause and effect, the research should not conclude causality.

INTERNET RESOURCES

www.stat.ufl.edu/vlib/statistics.html

This website of the University of Florida is linked to universities, statistical journals, mailing lists, and statistical software vendors. It is an excellent site for resource and reference information related to correlation.

http://dir.yahoo.com/science/mathematics/statistics

This Yahoo website offers links to some of the most popular statistics links on the internet. In addition, it provides links to statistics journals and online software.

www.amstat.org

This website of the American Statistical Association offers updated information about the field of statistics, professional journals, professional development courses, and careers.

www.analyze-it.com

This website provides a free 30-day download of the Analyze-it software package. Analyze-it is an add-in for Microsoft Excel (for Windows) and is designed to calculate correlation coefficients, along with other statistical calculations that are covered in this text.

REFERENCES

Christmann, E. P., and J. L. Badgett. 2000. *A four-year analytic comparison of eleventh grade academic achievement in the Slippery Rock Area High School, and district pupil expenditures.* Research report presented to The Slippery Rock School District's Board of Directors and The Pennsylvania Department of Education. (ERIC Document No. ED443824)

FURTHER READING

American Educational Research Association (AERA). 1999. *Standards for educational and psychological testing.* Washington, DC: American Educational Research Association.

Elmore, P. B., and P. L. Woehlke. 1997. *Basic statistics.* New York: Longman.

Gravetter, F. J., and L.B. Wallnau. 2002. *Essentials of statistics for the behavioral sciences.* New York: West.

Pearson, E. S. 1968. Some early correspondence between W. S. Gosset, R. A. Fischer, and Karl Pearson, with notes and comments. In *Studies in the history of statistics and probability,* eds. E. S. Pearson and M. G. Kendall. Vol. 1, pp. 405–417. London: Charles Griffin.

Raymond, J. C. 1999. *Statistical analysis in the behavioral sciences.* New York: McGraw-Hill.

Thorne, B. M., and J. M. Giesen. 2000. *Statistics for the behavioral sciences.* Mountain View, CA: Mayfield.

Zawojewski, J. S., and J. M. Shaughnessy. 2000. Mean and median: Are they really so easy? *Mathematics Teaching in the Middle School* 5 (7): 436–440.

Chapter 6

VALIDITY
OBJECTIVES

When you complete this chapter, you should be able to
1. compare and contrast the different types of validity,
2. calculate the validity of a test,
3. apply the validity of test results to classroom teaching,
4. apply validity to educational practices in school settings, and
5. determine the validity of a standardized test.

Key Terms

When you complete this chapter, you should be able to understand the following terms:

concurrent validity	face validity
construct validity	predictive validity
content validity	validity

Validity refers to the degree to which a student's score on a test is an accurate assessment of that student's knowledge or ability. For example, a student's score on a test consisting of two-digit addition examples is probably a valid measure of that student's ability to add two-digit numbers. On the other hand, a test consisting of one-digit addition examples would be a less valid measure of a student's ability to add two-digit numbers. If a test is a valid measure, you can use it to determine what students have learned as a result of classroom instruction.

Standardized achievement test results, such as the Iowa Tests of Basic Skills (ITBS), have been validated by researchers. If, for example, a student's ITBS mathematics score improves from fourth to fifth grade, we are confident that the scores increased because the student learned the material that was tested. The school district is assured that the instructional program offered for this student is working successfully. If an individual student or an entire group of students' ITBS scores decline, however, the school district needs to determine whether something has gone wrong with the instructional program—possibly outdated textbooks, teaching the wrong content, or even poor classroom management.

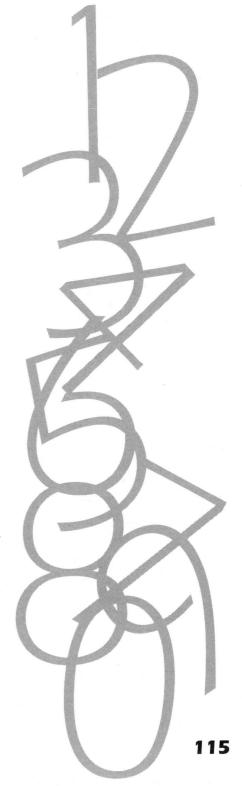

The concept of validity pertains to the interpretation of test results, as opposed to the test itself. In other words, we can say, as we did in the previous paragraphs, that our use of a particular test score, for a particular purpose, is valid. For example, if you want to measure your students' understanding of word analysis, you can examine their results from the ITBS Word Analysis section. Then, based on these test results, you can make teaching decisions either for an individual student or for large groups of students. You might decide, for example, to integrate additional word analysis strategies into your instruction if the entire class ITBS Word Analysis scores are low. Validity is used to make inferences based on the basis of test scores.

Validity is primarily a statistical concept that is based on a correlation (see Chapter 5). Exactly like correlation, validity is reported numerically with validity coefficients that range from +1.00 to 0.00 (positive validity coefficient) and 0.00 to -1.00 (negative validity coefficient). Because a negative validity coefficient at any level signifies an invalid test result, we are interested only in positive validity coefficients. A test with a validity coefficient of +0.9 would be said to be highly valid. To calculate a validity coefficient, we will use the same method we used to calculate the Pearson correlation coefficient (see Chapter 5).

In this chapter, we will describe the four types of validity: construct validity, content validity, concurrent validity, and predictive validity. Depending on the test and the rationale or purpose for its administration, an understanding of the different types of validity can give teachers useful information about students' test results. Moreover, if test results are going to be used to help make educational policy decisions, a knowledge of validity will give teachers and educational planners a more scientific basis for measuring student achievement. Therefore, to be more confident in the systematic and empirical interpretation of test results, teachers should understand the four types of validity.

CONSTRUCT VALIDITY

Construct validity is based on how closely a test measures a theoretical construction about the nature of human behavior. It is the degree of accuracy between a test's score and the construct a test is designed to measure. *Theoretical constructions* are sets of facts and principles that encompass our thinking about a complex idea. Some examples of theoretical constructions are intelligence, personality, and creativity. We use constructs when we attempt to define and measure complex traits, like intelligence. On a simpler level, you need a construct for "vocabulary" before you can try to determine if a student's vocabulary is large enough for the student to read at a third-grade level. A test developer for example, would need a construct for intelligence before developing an intelligence test. An advertiser would need to define a frequent shopper before deciding if a particular product appeals to frequent shoppers.

As an example, after creating a test, researchers write and test hypotheses related to the behavior of test takers with high or low scores. This process continues until the theory can be explained by the test's results. A simple way of determining construct validity is to correlate a test's results with the results of a reputable test that has established construct validity. For example, we would expect the Stanford-Binet intelligence test to correlate more highly with the Wechsler intelligence test than with reaction-time tests.

On the basis of how test results correspond with the forecasted theoretical goals of researchers, test developers continually refine test instruments. For example, a scientific breakthrough could cause the researchers responsible for a test to revise it. This is because construct validity is central to the other three types of validity. As we explore the other types of validity, keep in mind that since construct validity encompasses all of the other types of validity, it must be present for any other type of validity to exist.

CHECK FOR UNDERSTANDING

6.1.   What are the four types of validity?

6.2.   What is the numerical range of a validity coefficient?

6.3.   What does it mean when we say that without construct validity, the other types of validity cannot exist? Give an example.

CONTENT VALIDITY

Content validity means that the results of a test or other assessment instrument measure the content that was taught. Classroom teachers should clearly state what content is included when they prepare their unit and daily lesson plan objectives and make sure that the individual items on the test refer to this content. For example, when your lesson objective is that students be able to subtract whole numbers, an appropriate question based on this objective is asking the students to subtract seven from nine. If the emphasis of the subject matter is on the subtraction of two-digit numbers and the test is heavily weighted with single-digit addition problems, the test would have low content validity.

Content validity involves professional judgments. Your determination of the content validity of a test is always based on the subject matter. It is not always based on the calculation of a validity coefficient, as are predictive validity and concurrent validity, which we will discuss later. The two types of content validity are face validity and sampling validity.

Face Validity

Face validity, the least rigorous measurement of validity, is a subjective judgment that focuses on whether a test appears to cover the content that has been taught and is now being measured. Face validity is not accompanied by any supporting evidence, such as a validity coefficient. Because people making claims of face validity are not necessarily experts in assessment, face validity is sometimes referred to as "armchair" validity (Allen and Yen 1979).

The following scenario is an example of low face validity. A fifth-grade teacher in an urban elementary school gives students an arithmetic test designed to measure the students' knowledge of addition and subtraction. The test questions, however, are a series of word problems about buying produce at a farmer's market making the face validity of this test questionable.

Whether you construct a test or use a test supplied by a publisher, you should inspect the test items to make certain that the test measures what it purports to measure. Then, after the test is constructed, you should examine the test to determine whether it seems to have face validity. If a test lacks face validity, students may not have confidence in it and may not be motivated to put forth their maximum efforts. Keep in mind that face validity can never serve as a replacement for sampling validity, which will be discussed next.

Sampling Validity

Sampling validity, sometimes referred to as *logical validity*, is a more sophisticated form of face validity. To determine sampling validity, you match a representative sample of test questions to the instructional objectives that have been taught. Sampling validity comes from expert judgments. For example, a teacher could consult with a curriculum specialist or a college professor to determine the representativeness of the chosen set of items.

Although sampling validity is usually associated with standardized tests, it can also be used with teacher-generated tests. For example, a teacher is assessing an eighth-grade science unit on simple machines. The content to be tested includes all the daily lesson plan objectives taught to the students throughout the entire unit. If the teacher had taught a series of 10 lessons on simple machines, the test should include a representative sample of test items based on the lesson plan objectives. If the total number of test items is proportional to the objectives included in the curriculum, then we would say that the test has sampling validity, which signifies that it is content valid.

The unit consisted of a series of lessons on simple machines, covering levers, pulleys, and inclined planes. The teacher wants to construct a test that has 50 questions. Approximately 33% of the test items should be based on the content objectives related to levers, approximately 33% of the test items should be based on the content objectives related to pulleys, and approximately 33% of the test items should be based on the content objectives related to inclined planes. Table 6.1 shows how a teacher might construct a test that follows these guidelines for measuring student achievement on these objectives according to the levels of Bloom's Taxonomy.

Table 6.1

Teacher Plan for a Test on Simple Machines

Bloom's Taxonomy Level	Content Objectives		
	Levers	Pulleys	Inclined Planes
Knowledge	3	3	3
Application	3	3	3
Comprehension	3	2	3
Analysis	3	3	3
Synthesis	2	2	2
Evaluation	3	3	3

The columns of the grid categorize the test items by content area (levers, pulleys, or inclined planes). The rows of the grid show how many test items in each content area should be written at each different level of Bloom's Taxonomy. Using the grid allows the teacher to check that he or she included a representative sample of all content areas and all instructional levels on the test, which ensures that the test will have content validity. The grid can be adapted for use by elementary and secondary teachers for a test in any content area.

Establishing Content Validity

Content validity is used to determine how an assessment measures the outcomes of instruction. It is determined by expert judgments, which determine whether or not test items represent the behavioral objectives. Remember, face validity is a much more informal examination of test items and does not use an expert's judgment in its determination. Sampling validity, which relies on expert opinion, however, covers a representative sample of test questions relevant to the content domain.

Quantifying Content Validity

To determine content validity, you will need to identify content experts who are able to review the test questions before you administer the test. An expert should have a terminal degree in his or her field and have job-related experience in the profession. As an example, to determine what children need to know in science, the National Research Council established the National Committee on Science Education Standards and Assessment, which consists of a panel of experts who hold positions as professors of science education, state-level science supervisors, district-level science supervisors, scientists, and distinguished leaders from the scientific fields of medicine, engineering, physics, chemistry, geology, and biology.

Content Validity Ratio (CVR)

Over the years, methods for the quantification of content validity have been developed. We have adapted Lawshe's (1975) equation to quantify content validity in a classroom setting. The first step is to create a committee of raters to judge the content validity of each test or assessment item. (We recommend a committee of three members.) Next, each rater on the committee should answer the following question for each test item:

Is the skill or knowledge measured by this item
- essential to measure the behavioral objective?
- useful but not essential to measure the behavioral objective?
- not necessary to measure the behavioral objective?

After the committee members have answered the CVR question for each item, the next step is to tally the number of committee members who responded "essential" for each individual test item. After the responses are tallied for each individual item, a CVR can be calculated for each item by using Equation 6.1.

	Equation 6.1
$CVR = \dfrac{ne - n/2}{n/2}$	

In the equation, ne = the number of committee members indicating "essential" and n = the number of committee members. According to Lawshe, a minimum CVR ratio of 0.99 is required for a committee of three to seven members for an item to be considered content valid. In this case, all three committee members would have to agree that the item is essential for it to be deemed content valid. With eight committee members, however, a 0.75 CVR provides acceptable content validity. It is safe to say that the more committee members involved in the process, the lower the acceptable CVR (see Lawshe for further information).

Finding a Qualified Expert

A classroom teacher can ask school district personnel who are employed as content area "directors" of subjects such as mathematics, science, and reading to serve as qualified experts to review their classroom assessments. Although this method is not as comprehensive as that employed by the National Committee on Science Education Standards and Assessment, it is nevertheless a good way to screen test items, test directions, test layout, and test scoring before the test or assessment is administered to students.

CHECK FOR UNDERSTANDING

6.4. How are face validity and sampling validity different?

6.5. Based on the grade level and subject area that you will be teaching, create a teacher plan for a content unit and classroom test.

6.6. Is it possible for test takers to be judges of face validity? Explain your answer.

6.7. Why is it important for teachers to determine the sampling validity of tests provided by textbook companies?

CONCURRENT VALIDITY

The *concurrent validity* of test results is the extent to which students' scores on a new test correspond to their scores on an established test. To determine the concurrent validity of test results, one test's results are compared to another test's results, with both tests being based on the same or a similar construct. Thus, one test is used to estimate the results of another test, with the results of the second test being known as the criterion measure. The time between the two tests can range from one day to one week.

The use of concurrent validity is justified when performance on one test is used to estimate performance on a second test at the same time. For example, if a school counselor is interested in measuring the intelligence of a large group of students, it might not be practical to administer the Stanford-Binet Intelligence Test because this instrument is an individual test. An individual test necessitates a one-on-one relationship between examiner and examinee, whereas a group test can be administered to two or more individuals simultaneously. If it would save time and money to administer a group intelligence test to a collection of students, use a group test such as the Cognitive Abilities Test (CAT), which would save instructional time for the teachers and students and save money for the school district. In this case, if the CAT has acceptable concurrent validity with the Stanford-Binet Intelligence Test, the CAT may be used as an alternate means for estimating intelligence. Remember, however, that an individual intelligence test almost always provides a more accurate estimate of intelligence than to a group test.

To be considered useful, concurrent validity coefficients should be above 0.60 for education purposes. Therefore, any concurrent validity coefficient below 0.60 means that a test should be considered questionable.

Hence, it is important that you establish concurrent validity before using a new test to match performance on an established test. To calculate a concurrent validity coefficient, you would need to calculate a correlation calculation between subjects' scores from the established criterion, the Stanford-Binet Intelligence Test, and the new test, the CAT. Table 6.2 gives the data necessary to determine the concurrent validity of scores on the two tests. Calculation 6.1 shows how to calculate the concurrent validity. (See also Chapter 5, "The Pearson Correlation Coefficient," p. 98, to understand Table 6.2 more fully.)

Table 6.2

Concurrent Validity Data

Student	Stanford-Binet Individual Test (x)	CAT Group Test (y)	$z_x = (x - \bar{x})/S_x$	$z_y = (y - \bar{y})/S_y$	$z_x z_y$
Robert	95.000	115	-.736	.149	-.110
Susan	101.000	85	-.449	-1.059	.475
Alfred	115.000	135	.220	.954	.210
Kendra	84.000	71	-1.261	-1.622	2.046
Rebecca	129.000	118	.888	.270	.240
Fritzie	88.000	101	-1.070	-.415	.444
Kay	108.000	90	-.115	-.857	.098
Alfonzo	138.000	152	1.318	1.638	2.160
Jeff	145.000	131	1.653	.793	1.311
Bob	101.000	115	-.449	.149	-.067
	$\bar{x} = 110.4$ $S_x = 20.93$	$\bar{y} = 111.3$ $S_y = 24.84$			$\sum z_x z_y = 6.806$

Calculation 6.1

$$r = \frac{\sum z_x z_y}{n - 1}$$

or

$$r = \frac{6.806}{10 - 1} = 0.756$$

Calculation 6.1 shows that r = 0.756, which translates to a strong positive concurrent validity coefficient between the Stanford-Binet Group Intelligence Test and the CAT. Although the validity coefficient is strong, it is below 0.60, and therefore it is not acceptable to use the CAT group test as a substitute for the Stanford-Binet Group Intelligence Individual Test.

CHECK FOR UNDERSTANDING

6.8. In your own words, explain concurrent validity.

6.9. Calculate a concurrent validity coefficient for the data given in Table 6.3.

Table 6.3

Data From Two Standardized IQ Tests Given During the Same Week

Student	Wechsler Individual Test (x)	CAT Group Test (y)
Phil	93	95
Sally	100	98
Frank	130	128
Alice	74	71
Gertrude	120	122
Ellen	81	84
Nancy	103	104
Julio	145	144
Tom	96	94
Matthew	89	87

6.10.   Based on the calculated validity coefficient, would you recommend that the CAT Group IQ Test be used as a replacement for the Wechsler Individual IQ Test? Why or why not?

6.11.   How is concurrent validity different from content validity?

6.12.   Calculate a CVR for a test item where four of five committee members have judged an item as essential to measure the behavioral objective. Does this item have acceptable content validity?

PREDICTIVE VALIDITY

Predictive validity refers to the degree to which a test score predicts future behavior. We determine predictive validity by calculating the correlation between a test score and the test taker's future behavior. The most common use of predictive validity is for the interpretation of aptitude test results. For example, all aptitude tests, including the SAT and ACT, and intelligence tests such as the Stanford-Binet and the Wechsler tests, rely on predictive validity. Aptitude tests are designed to assess human potential and are usually administered as standardized tests that attempt to measure logical reasoning. Logical reasoning can be subcategorized into the following: (1) verbal reasoning, (2) numerical reasoning, and (3) spatial reasoning. Verbal reasoning measures the understanding of written text; numerical reasoning measures the understanding of numbers, algebra, and quadratic equations; and spatial reasoning measures the understanding of the geometry of shapes and patterns.

Determining Predictive Validity

To determine *predictive validity* you administer a test and associate the test's results with a criterion measure. In this case, the criterion measure is the behavior that the test results attempt to predict. The next step is to calculate a correlation coefficient to compare the initial test results (the predictive measure) to the criterion measure. Thus, if a group of 12th graders takes the SAT at the beginning of its senior year, those results can be used to predict future college achievement. As an example, let's look at the verbal (now called critical reading) SAT scores of a group of 12th graders (keep in mind that SAT scores range from a low of 200 to a high of 800). SAT verbal scores have been construct validated to measure verbal reasoning, the ability to understand written text. To establish the predictive validity of the verbal SAT scores, which is our predictor, we need to use college English achievement as our criterion. To calculate predictive validity, we would match the verbal SAT results of the 12th graders to their college freshman English grades (see Table 6.4).

Table 6.4

Calculating Predictive Validity

Student	SAT Verbal Score	Freshman English Grades (%)	$z_x = (x - \bar{x})/s_x$	$z_y = (y - \bar{y})/s_y$	$z_x z_y$
Karl	650	93	1.094	1.169	1.279
Susan	420	69	-1.133	-0.879	0.996
Frank	700	95	1.578	1.340	2.115
Sally	500	84	-0.358	0.401	-0.144
Roxanne	370	57	-1.617	-1.903	3.077
Hemings	580	70	0.416	-0.794	-0.331
Ray	480	76	-0.552	-0.282	0.156
Julio	610	88	0.707	0.742	0.524
Jackson	490	81	-0.455	0.145	-0.066
Virginia	570	80	0.319	0.060	0.019
	$\bar{x} = 537$ $S_x = 103.29$	$\bar{y} = 79.3$ $S_y = 11.72$			$\sum z_x z_y = 7.625$

For predictive validity to be considered useful for education purposes, coefficients should be above 0.60, which is the base rate for predictive validity according to Taylor and Russell (1939). Any predictive validity coefficient below 0.60 would probably not be considered useful. To calculate a predictive validity coefficient, we determine the correlation between the students' SAT verbal scores and the criterion, their freshman English grades (see Table 6.4).

Calculation 6.2 shows that r = 0.847, which translates to a very strong positive concurrent validity coefficient between the SAT verbal scores and the college English grades. Therefore, we can conclude that SAT verbal scores are good predictors of college English achievement.

$$r = \frac{\sum z_x z_y}{n - 1}$$

or

$$r = \frac{7.625}{10 - 1} = 0.847$$

Calculation 6.2

CALCULATOR EXPLORATION

Using the TI-73, TI-83, or TI-84, you can easily compute a validity coefficient by following these keystrokes.

TI-73

Step 1. Display list editor by pressing LIST. Here, you can enter up to 999 elements. Under L1, list all of the scores from the SAT that are listed in Table 6.4. Next, under L2, list all of the scores listed under Freshman English Grades in Table 6.4.

Step 2. Press 2nd LIST to activate STAT. Next, scroll to the right and select CALC. Next, scroll down to 5: LinReg (ax+b), press 5, then press ENTER.

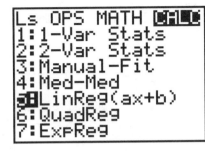

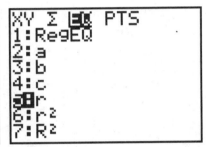

Step 3. Press 2nd APPS to activate VARS. Next, scroll down to 3: Statistics and press 3. Next, scroll over to EQ and scroll down to 5: r, select 5, and press ENTER. Press ENTER again to get the validity coefficient.

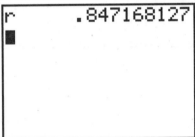

TI-83/84

Step 1. First press STAT. Next, select 1: Edit by pressing 1. Here you can enter up to 999 elements. Under L1, list all of the scores from the SAT that are listed in Table 6.4. Next, under L2, list all of the scores listed under Percentage English Grades in Table 6.4.

L1	L2	L3	2
650	93	------	
420	69		
700	95		
500	84		
370	57		
580	70		
480	76		

L2(1)=93

Interpreting Assessment Data

Step 2. Press STAT and scroll to the right and select CALC. Next, scroll down to 4: LinReg (ax+b), press 4, and press ENTER.

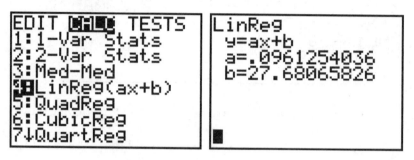

Step 3. Press VARS. Next, scroll down to 5: Statistics and press 5. Next, scroll over to EQ. Next, scroll down to 7: r, and press 7. Press ENTER again to get the validity coefficient.

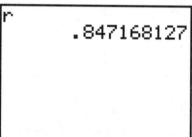

MAXIMIZING VALIDITY

In an effort to maximize the validity of test results, you should try to minimize the factors that can decrease this validity. Therefore, you should check a test before you administer it. The Test Administration Checklist in Table 6.5 will help you maximize the validity of the tests you administer.

Table 6.5

Test Administration Checklist

Test Administration Variables	(√) If satisfactory
1. Motivated students and minimized test anxiety prior to test administration	
2. Presented students with clear directions indicating how students should respond to the test questions	
3. Provided an adequate sample of test questions that measure all of the appropriate content domains	
4. Gave an adequate amount of time to complete the examination	
5. Minimized test question bias so that students are not put at a disadvantage	
6. Test has a representative sample of test questions (between 50 and 100 test questions)	
7. Correct multiple-choice and true-false responses are randomly placed so that the students do not identify a pattern—can be determined by roll of a die or toss of a coin	
8. Least difficult items are placed at the beginning of the test with a progression of more difficult items toward the end of the test	
9. Vocabulary and test item sentence structure are appropriate to the test takers	
10. Test taking environment is suitable for maximum success—proper lighting, minimal noise and interruptions, adequate desk space	
11. Completed a test item analysis on the test results to get the percentage of items answered correctly	

CHECK FOR UNDERSTANDING

6.13.   Define predictive validity.

6.14.   Explain the similarities and differences between concurrent validity and predictive validity.

6.15.   Based on the data in Table 6.6, calculate a predictive validity coefficient and interpret the results.

Table 6.6

Graduate Record Exam (GRE) Scores and Graduate Statistics Grades

Student	GRE (Math) Scores	Graduate School Statistics Grades
Matthew	710	95
Mary	780	98
Sarah	420	65
John	500	71
Abraham	380	50
Benjy	210	48
Abner	103	104
Luke	410	69
Jeb	650	88
Theresa	550	81

6.16. Using the internet and/or your university library, research some standardized tests that are designed to predict future academic performance—for example, SAT, ACT, GRE, MCAT, LSAT, and MAT. Were you able to find a validity coefficient for the test that you researched? If so, what is the reported validity coefficient for the instrument that you selected? What other information did the test developer provide about this evaluation instrument?

IN SUMMARY

Validity is a way to determine whether or not our measurements are on target. The validity of test results is based on evidence that relates to construct validity, content validity, concurrent validity, and predictive validity. Construct validity is a theoretical construction for items such as intelligence, personality, or creativity. Content validity, divided into face validity and sampling validity, is concerned with how well the sample of test questions represents the instructional objectives. Concurrent validity compares one test's results to another test's results, when both tests are taken at nearly the same time. Predictive validity relates the test results of test takers to future behaviors. The next chapter will address the issue of reliability, which is associated with validity and is a tool for measuring the consistency of test results.

CHAPTER REVIEW QUESTIONS

6.17. You are teaching high school geometry. During your fourth year as a classroom teacher, you decide to create a new final exam, designed to take less time for your students to finish. How would you determine that the new exam has concurrent validity in relation to the exam you used in the past? How would you decide whether to use the new test? Explain. Based on the test results in Table 6.7, calculate a concurrent validity coefficient for the data.

Table 6.7

Geometry Scores

Student	Final Exam (Old Version)	Final Exam (New Version)
1	77	61
2	67	72
3	56	77
4	99	97
5	83	88
6	74	78
7	100	70
8	74	78
9	73	80
10	69	71

6.18. Based on the concurrent validity coefficient that was calculated from the data in Table 6.7, do you recommend the new test over the old test? Please explain your answer.

6.19. Which of the following predictive validity coefficients would be the most useful in predicting future performance?
a. 0.33
b. 0.60
c. 0.85
d. 1.10

6.20. Which of the following concurrent validity coefficients would be the least useful in predicting future behavior?
a. 0.33
b. 0.60
c. 0.85
d. 1.10

6.21. Which type of validity matches test items with behavioral objectives?
a. Construct validity
b. Content validity
c. Concurrent validity
d. Predictive validity

6.22. Which type of validity would be used for comparing a test of quantitative reasoning with college algebra achievement?
a. Construct validity
b. Content validity
c. Concurrent validity
d. Predictive validity

6.23. Which type of validity would be used for comparing a new version of an IQ test with an established version of an IQ test?
a. Construct validity
b. Content validity
c. Concurrent validity
d. Predictive validity

6.24. Which type of validity is based on a theoretical construct like anxiety, intelligence, or spatial creative abilities?
a. Construct validity
b. Content validity
c. Concurrent validity
d. Predictive validity

6.25. Name several tests that are designed to predict future behavior.

6.26. Based on the data in Table 6.8, calculate a predictive validity coefficient for SAT math section scores and freshman calculus grades. Explain whether SAT results are a good predictor of freshman calculus grades.

Table 6.8

Scholastic Assessment Test (SAT) Math Scores and Freshman Calculus Grades

Student	SAT (Math) Scores	Freshman Calculus Grades
1	610	85
2	720	98
3	520	75
4	600	81
5	380	50
6	510	78
7	420	68
8	510	79
9	610	88
10	450	71

ANSWERS: CHECK FOR UNDERSTANDING

6.1. Construct, content, concurrent, and predictive

6.2. -1.00 to $+1.00$

6.3. Because construct validity encompasses all the other types of validity, it must be present for any other type of validity to exist.

6.4. Face validity is informal and usually involves the test taker, whereas sampling validity takes into account the behavioral objectives as they correspond to the test items.

6.5. Responses will vary; however, please make sure that the relevant National Standards (e.g., NSTA, NCTM, etc.) are cited and that there is an adequate sample of test questions that correspond with the objectives.

6.6. Yes, because, as mentioned earlier, "people making claims of face validity are not necessarily experts in assessment, face validity is sometimes referred to as 'arm chair' validity" (Allen and Yen 1979).

6.7. To assure that the appropriate content is being taught and that they are confident in what is being measured

6.8. The extent to which students' scores on a new test correspond to their scores on an established test

6.9. $r = 0.995$

6.10. Because the calculated validity coefficient is (r) = 0.995, it would be acceptable to replace the Wechsler Individual IQ Test with the CAT. However, validity coefficients this high have not been calculated with large pools of data.

6.11. Concurrent validity compares the results of an established test to the results of a new test. Content validity, however, is based on the extent to which a measurement reflects the specific intended domain of content. Therefore, concurrent validity is concerned with the mathematical relationship between two variables and content validity is concerned with how well the items on a test reflect the content.

6.12. The content validity ratio (CVR) is 0.60, which equals the 0.60 base rate of Taylor and Russell (1939).

6.13. Predictive validity refers to the degree to which a test score predicts future behavior. We determine predictive validity by calculating the correlation between a test score and the test taker's future behavior.

6.14. The procedure for calculating the two types of validity is mathematically identical. However, predictive validity is concerned with the prediction of a future behavior and concurrent validity compares a new test result to an old test result.

6.15. The predictive validity correlation is (r) = 0.375, which is not useful for education because it is below 0.60, the base rate for predictive validity according to Taylor and Russell (1939).

6.16. The answers to this question will vary; however, the results should be higher than 0.60 for the instruments mentioned in this question.

ANSWERS: CHAPTER REVIEW QUESTIONS

6.17. Answers will vary to the first part of the question. The concurrent validity coefficient is (r) = 0.345.

6.18. Since the coefficient is below a 0.600, you should not recommend the new test.

6.19. c. 0.85

6.20. a. 0.33

6.21. b. Content validity

6.22. d. Predictive validity

6.23. c. Concurrent validity

6.24. a. Construct validity

6.25. Because high-stakes tests must have high predictive validity, the GRE, SAT, MCAT, and LSAT, tests designed to predict behavior, must conform to that standard.

6.26. The predictive validity coefficient is (r) = 0.9416, which represents a very acceptable level for predicting freshman calculus grades from SAT math scores.

INTERNET RESOURCES

www.collegeboard.com

The website of the College Board, the organization that administers the SAT and many other standardized tests, includes sample items, test descriptions, and other useful information for students. Because many students use this site, teachers should be familiar with the information it contains and be prepared to answer students' questions and correct their misinterpretations.

www.ets.com

The website of the Educational Testing Service, the organization that governs the College Board and administers a variety of tests such as the PRAXIS, GRE, Advanced Placement Tests, and includes sample items, test descriptions, and other useful information for students.

www.act.org

This is the site of the American College Testing Program, which produces the ACT Assessment. This ACT is designed to assess high school students' general educational development and their abilities to complete college-level work. This site includes information about the ACT and all other tests produced by the American College Testing Service.

www.gre.org/textonly/reswrit.html

This Graduate Record Exam site offers several links related to test validity. In addition, it has several downloadable research articles on test validity that may enhance your understanding of test validity.

www.ed.gov/offices/OUS/PES/primer6.html

This section of the U.S. Department of Education website gives a brief summary of test validity and reliability.

www.apa.org/science/faq-findtests.html

The American Psychological Association website contains information about published psychological tests—those available for purchase through a test publisher. It includes tips on how to locate tests within a given subject area, how to contact the test publisher once you find an appropriate test, and where to find computerized testing materials and information.

A second section focuses on unpublished psychological tests and measures—those that are not available commercially for purchase. Information about unpublished tests usually appears in journal articles. The test can usually be obtained directly from the researcher who created the test or measure. This section tells you how to find unpublished tests in your area of interest and highlights your responsibilities as a user of unpublished psychological tests.

REFERENCES

Allen, M. J., and W. M. Yen. 1979. *Introduction to measurement theory.* Prospect Heights, IL: Waveland.

American Educational Research Association (AERA), American Psychological Association (APA), and National Council on Measurement in Education (NCME). 1999. *Standards for educational and psychological testing, 3rd ed.* Washington, DC: Author.

Bloom, B. S. 1956. *Taxonomy of educational objectives, Handbook 1: Cognitive domain.* New York: David McKay.

Lawshe, C.H. 1975. A quantitative approach to content validity. *Personnel Psychology* 28: 563–575.

Taylor, H. C., and J. T. Russell. 1939. The relationship of validity coefficients to the practical effectiveness of tests in selection: Discussion and tables. *Journal of Applied Psychology* 23: 565–578.

FURTHER READING

Christmann, E. P., and J. L. Badgett. 2000. *A four-year analytic comparison of eleventh grade academic achievement in the Slippery Rock Area High School, and district pupil expenditures.* Research report presented to The Slippery Rock School District's Board of Directors and The Pennsylvania Department of Education. (ERIC Document No. ED443824)

Cronbach, L. J., and P. Meehl. 1955. Construct validity in psychological tests. *Psychological Bulletin* 52: 281–302.

Elmore, P. B., and P. L. Woehlke. 1997. *Basic statistics.* New York: Longman.

Gravetter, F. J., and L. B. Wallnau. 2002. *Essentials of statistics for the behavioral sciences.* New York: West.

Raymondu, J. C. 1999. *Statistical analysis in the behavioral sciences.* New York: McGraw Hill.

Thorndike, R. L., and E. P. Hagen. 1978. *The cognitive abilities test.* Lombard, IL: Riverside.

Thorne, B. M., and J. M. Giesen. 2000. *Statistics for the behavioral sciences*. Mountain View, CA: Mayfield.

Zawojewski, J. S., and J. M. Shaughnessy. 2000. Mean and median: Are they really so easy? *Mathematics Teaching in the Middle School* 5 (7): 436–440.

Chapter 7

RELIABILITY

OBJECTIVES

When you complete this chapter, you should be able to
1. compare and contrast the different types of reliability,
2. calculate the reliability of test results,
3. demonstrate an understanding of standard error of measurement,
4. apply reliability to education practices in school settings, and
5. determine the reliability of a standardized test.

Key Terms

When you complete this chapter, you should be able to understand
equivalent forms method   split-halves method
Kuder-Richardson method   standard error of measurement
reliability   test-retest validity

RELIABILITY AND VALIDITY

In essence, reliability is the consistency of test results. To understand the meaning of reliability and how it relates to validity, imagine going to an airport to take flight #007 from Pittsburgh to San Diego. If, every time the airplane makes the flight, the passengers are dropped off in Dallas, Flight #007 is not making it to its target destination. Therefore, it is not a valid claim for the airlines to advertise that flight #007 takes passengers from Pittsburgh to San Diego. If flight #007 goes from Pittsburgh to Dallas consistently, however, the flight is reliable, even though it takes passengers to the wrong destination.

Similarly, test results may be reliable but invalid. For example, students are given a mathematics test that lacks content validity; in other words, the test does not test the content that was taught. The results can be reliable in that the scores are consistent, but the test is not measuring the desired content. It is reliable but invalid.

Consider flight #007 again. Suppose it consistently flies from Pittsburgh to San Diego and reaches the target destination each

time. Now, because flight #007 consistently makes the trip to its target destination, the flight is both highly reliable and valid. In educational testing, if a test's results are highly consistent and measure what the instrument is targeted to evaluate, the results are considered both reliable and valid. Whether we are talking about major airline flights, a local school district's testing program results, or an individual teacher's final exam results, the goal is to have results that are both reliable (highly consistent) and valid (measurably on target).

Now imagine that flight #007 from Pittsburgh to San Diego randomly lands in destinations scattered throughout the United States—perhaps Boston, Seattle, Miami, and Phoenix. There is no consistency in where the plane lands, and it misses its target destination each time. It is neither reliable nor valid. Similarly, test results that are inconsistent and do not measure what they are designed to measure are neither reliable nor valid.

Finally, if flight #007 from Pittsburgh to San Diego reaches San Diego 50% of the time, there is a measurable level of validity and reliability in that the flight reaches San Diego, its target, with some consistency 50% of the time. Reliability must be prevalent for validity to be possible. If the airplane reaches the target destination 50% of the time, we have a measurable level of reliability and validity—it may not be acceptable, but it is measurable. As with an airline flight destination, the level of reliability affects the level of validity in educational testing, which will be addressed throughout the remainder of this chapter.

RELIABILITY AND VALIDITY REQUIREMENTS

Rule #1—Test results that have high reliability can have low validity.

Rule #2—Test results that have high reliability can have high validity.

Rule #3—Test results that have low reliability cannot have high validity.

Rule #4—Test results that have high validity cannot have low reliability.

THE RELIABILITY COEFFICIENT

The two previous chapters discussed the topics of correlation and validity. Similar to the Pearson correlation coefficient, reliability coefficients are mathematical calculations that range between -1.0 and $+1.0$. Depending on the situation, however, there are several ways to calculate a reliability coefficient. A *reliability coefficient* is an estimate of the reliability of test results. The following sections will examine the methods for estimating the reliability of test results.

CHECK FOR UNDERSTANDING
7.1.   Is it possible to have high reliability with low validity? Explain.
7.2.   What is the numerical range of a reliability coefficient?
7.3.   What is the difference between a reliability coefficient and a validity coefficient?

ESTIMATING THE RELIABILITY OF TEST RESULTS

Test-Retest Method

The *test-retest method* of estimating reliability (sometimes known as the *coefficient of stability*) is computed when the same group of students takes the same test on two different test administrations. As with concurrent validity, the time between test administrations can range from one day to a week. To calculate a reliability coefficient, match the pairs of scores from test #1 to those from test #2 (see Table 7.1). Next, after the scores have been paired, calculate a Pearson correlation between the results of test #1 and test #2.

Table 7.1

Test-Retest Method: Calculating a Reliability Coefficient

Student	Test #1 (x)	Test #2 (y)	$z_x = (x - \bar{x})/S_x$	$z_y = (y - \bar{y})/S_y$	$z_x z_y$
Susan	95.000	91.000	1.136	0.895	1.016
Joe	100.000	98.000	1.579	1.659	2.620
Harry	88.000	81.000	0.515	-0.196	-0.101
Elizabeth	84.000	89.000	0.160	0.677	0.108
Steve	79.000	74.000	-0.284	-0.960	0.273
Rob	88.000	92.000	0.515	1.004	0.517
Lionel	68.000	71.000	-1.260	-1.288	1.622
Debbie	65.000	74.000	-1.526	-0.960	1.465
Alfred	73.000	77.000	-0.816	-0.633	0.517
Mark	82.000	81.000	-0.018	-0.196	0.003
	$\bar{x} = 82.20$ $S_x = 11.272$	$\bar{y} = 82.80$ $S_y = 9.163$			$\sum z_x z_y = 8.040$

Table 7.1 shows how to calculate a reliability coefficient using the test-retest method. In this example, a teacher is determining the estimated reliability of a test based on the Battle of First Manassas by testing and retesting a group of ninth-grade social studies students. As with the calculation of the Pearson correlation coefficient, the definitional formula is used to show how to calculate the test-retest estimated reliability coefficient.

Calculation 7.1 shows that r = 0.893, which translates to a very strong positive reliability coefficient between the results of test #1 and test #2 for this test. We can conclude that, because the reliability coefficient is above 0.60, the test is acceptable for classroom use.

$$r = \frac{\sum z_x z_y}{n-1}$$

or

$$r = \frac{8.040}{10-1} = 0.893$$

Calculation 7.1

The test-retest method presents two major problems for the classroom teacher. The first problem is that students can go home after the first test administration and search for answers for the second test. The second problem is that the test-retest method uses additional instructional time for the two test administrations.

Alternate Forms Method

The alternate forms method of estimating reliability (sometimes known as the *measure of equivalence and stability*) uses two different tests with equivalent items. As with the test-retest method, the same group of students is tested on two different occasions. As with the test-retest method and concurrent validity, the time between test administrations can range from one day to a week. The length of the time between tests, however, can compromise the integrity of the reliability estimate because of changes in students' health, memory, mood, or similar factors. It is best to administer the second form of the test as soon as possible when fewer changes are likely to have taken place.

To calculate a reliability coefficient using the alternate-forms method, match the results from test #1 to the results of test #2. Next, calculate a Pearson correlation coefficient between the two sets of test scores. Table 7.2 shows a comparison between the two test administrations of the mathematics section of a final examination for a middle school science class. The computation shows the use of the Pearson correlation in calculating the alternate-forms method for estimating reliability.

Most companies that publish standardized tests have two or more equivalent forms of each test available. Therefore, the alternate-forms method can be used by teachers and test publishers to compute the estimated reliability of test results. It is essential that, before estimating the reliability with the alternate-forms method, you make sure that the test developer has established test-form equivalence. Otherwise, the information that the alternative-forms method yields is useless.

Table 7.2

Alternate Forms Method: Calculating a Reliability Coefficient for a Science Test Results

Student	Test #1 (x)	Test #2 (y)	$z_x = (x - \overline{x})/S_x$	$z_y = (y - \overline{y})/S_y$	$z_x z_y$
Fred	100	97	1.672	1.817	3.038
Rob	92	88	0.851	0.748	0.637
Mari	89	89	0.544	0.867	0.471
Joan	88	80	0.441	-0.202	-0.089
Carl	87	78	0.338	-0.439	-0.149
Jim	83	87	-0.072	0.629	-0.045
John	79	76	-0.482	-0.677	0.326
Harry	78	72	-0.585	-1.152	0.673
Louise	76	80	-0.790	-0.202	0.159
Mark	65	70	-1.918	-1.390	2.665
	$\overline{x} = 83.70$ $S_x = 9.75$	$\overline{y} = 81.70$ $S_y = 8.42$			$\sum z_x z_y = 7.687$

Calculation 7.2 shows that r = 0.854, which translates to a very strong positive reliability coefficient between the results of test #1 and test #2 of these middle school science tests. Once again, we can conclude that because the reliability coefficient is above 0.60, the test results are within an acceptable range for classroom use.

Calculation 7.2

$$r = \frac{\sum z_x z_y}{n - 1}$$

or

$$r = \frac{7.687}{10 - 1} = 0.854$$

The Split-Halves Method

The *split-halves method*, sometimes known as the *coefficient of internal consistency*, estimates reliability when the individual items of a test are compared with each other. In this case, a test is administered once to a single group of students. Then the test items are divided into two subtests, the odd-numbered items on one subtest and the even-numbered items on the other. Each student's total scores on the two subtests are compared to determine internal reliability. Table 7.3 shows how to create the two subtests from a single test for a single student. For simplicity, we are using only 20 questions for a fifth-grade test on rocks and minerals. The larger the number of items on a test, the more accurate the measure of internal reliability. As a rule of thumb, it is a good practice to use between 40 and 60 items on a test if you wish to measure internal reliability.

Table 7.3

Scoring Two Subtests From One Test Administration for a Single Student

Sum Odd Numbered Items	Sum Even Numbered Items
Question #1 [Correct]	Question #2 [Incorrect]
Question #3 [Correct]	Question #4 [Correct]
Question #5 [Incorrect]	Question #6 [Incorrect]
Question #7 [Correct]	Question #8 [Correct]
Question #9 [Correct]	Question #10 [Correct]
Question #11 [Incorrect]	Question #12 [Correct]
Question #13 [Correct]	Question #14 [Correct]
Question #15 [Correct]	Question #16 [Correct]
Question #17 [Correct]	Question #18 [Correct]
Question #19 [Correct]	Question #20 [Incorrect]
Total Correct = 8 Items	Total Correct = 7 Items

As you see in Table 7.3, because there are now two separate test scores from one single test administration, you can calculate two test scores for every student in the class. The next step is for you to collate the results of each student's odd-numbered items and each student's even-numbered items. Then, calculate the split-halves reliability coefficient by using the Pearson correlation coefficient (see Table 7.4a).

Table 7.4a

Collated Test Results for the Split-Halves Method

Student	Score on odd-numbered items	Score on even-numbered items
Tom	7	9
Sal	8	7
Barbara	3	6
Susan	9	10
Tammy	5	7
Joe	4	6
Ike	9	8
Pete	7	9
Irene	8	7
Sandra	9	7
Keshawn	7	8
Arlene	8	8
Eli	7	7
Mark	8	7
Agatha	9	8
Louis	6	9
Luke	8	8
William	10	10
Stacey	6	5
Heather	9	8
Byron	8	9

Once you have calculated each student's odd-numbered item and even-numbered item totals, use the definitional formula of the Pearson correlation coefficient, now being referred to as a reliability coefficient because it is used to estimate the test result reliability (see Table 7.4b).

Table 7.4b

Collated Test Results for the Split-Halves Method

Student	Score on odd-numbered items (x)	Score on even-numbered items (y)	$Z_x = (x - \overline{x})/S_x$	$Z_y = (y - \overline{y})/S_y$	$z_x z_y$
Tom	7	9	-0.215	0.952	-0.205
Sal	8	7	0.349	-0.586	-0.205
Barbara	3	6	-2.470	-1.355	3.347
Susan	9	10	0.913	1.722	1.571
Tammy	5	7	-1.342	-0.586	0.787
Joe	4	6	-1.906	-1.355	2.583
Ike	9	8	0.913	0.183	0.167
Pete	7	9	-0.215	0.952	-0.205
Irene	8	7	0.349	-0.586	-0.205
Sandra	9	7	0.913	-0.586	-0.535
Keshawn	7	8	-0.215	0.183	-0.039
Arlene	8	8	0.349	0.183	0.064
Eli	7	7	-0.215	-0.586	0.126
Mark	8	7	0.349	-0.586	-0.205
Agatha	9	8	0.913	0.183	0.167
Louis	6	9	-0.778	0.952	-0.741
Luke	8	8	0.349	0.183	0.064
William	10	10	1.476	1.722	2.542
Stacey	6	5	-0.778	-2.125	1.654
Heather	9	8	0.913	0.183	0.167
Byron	8	9	0.349	0.952	0.332
	$\overline{x} = 7.381$ $S_x = 1.774$	$\overline{y} = 7.762$ $S_y = 1.300$			$\sum z_x z_y = 11.231$

Calculation 7.3 shows that r = 0.562, which translates to a moderately positive reliability coefficient between the results of odd-numbered items and even-numbered items of this fifth-grade test on rocks and minerals.

$$r = \frac{\sum z_x z_y}{n - 1}$$

Calculation 7.3

or

$$r = \frac{11.231}{21 - 1} = 0.562$$

The calculated correlation of 0.562 from Calculation 7.3 is based on a comparison of two half assessments, each containing one-half the total number of test questions. Because of the small number of questions, the estimated reliability tends to be low. Therefore, the Spearman-Brown formula is used to correct the coefficient for the error caused by splitting the test in half. This formula will give us a theoretical reliability estimate that is closer to the actual reliability estimate for the full version of the test.

Equation 7.1 shows the formula for the Spearman-Brown formula where R_f = reliability for the full version of the test, and r = the calculated Pearson correlation estimate resulting from the split-halves method.

$$R_f = \frac{2 * r}{1 + r}$$

Equation 7.1

Now, using the data from Table 7.4b, we can calculate a more accurate estimate of reliability from the split-halves by using the Spearman-Brown formula. Calculation 7.4 shows how, after we calculate R_f with the Spearman-Brown formula, we arrive at a reliability of 0.720 for the full version of the test, as opposed to a split-half reliability estimate of 0.562. Therefore, we can conclude that because the reliability coefficient is above 0.60, the test results are within acceptable range for classroom use.

$$R_f = \frac{2 * 0.562}{1 + 0.562} = 0.720$$

Calculation 7.4

Kuder-Richardson K-R Formula

For the most part, the *Kuder-Richardson (K-R) method,* also known as the *method of rational equivalence,* is a better method of calculating a reliability estimate than are the test-retest method and the alternate-forms method because it is less time consuming. The split-halves method, however, has been known to give higher estimates of internal consistency. Richardson and Kuder derived several different formulas for their method (1939). The one we present here, known as K-R 21, is the most practical for classroom teachers to use. The formula to calculate the K-R 21 is found in Equation 7.2.

Equation 7.2

K-R 21 = Kuder-Richardson Formula 21: This formula is often useful for quick estimates of reliability given a limited amount of information.

To compute K-R 21, you need the following information:
K = the number of items on the test
M = the mean score on the test
s = the standard deviation of the scores on the test

$$\text{K-R 21} = \left(\frac{K}{K-1}\right)\left(1 - \frac{M(K-M)}{K*s^2}\right)$$

Note: s is the standard deviation of the test scores based on the mean of the test scores.

Table 7.5 shows how to calculate a reliability coefficient using the K-R 21 method for estimating the reliability of test results. In this example, a teacher is determining the estimated reliability of a high school English test that has 100 questions. As with the split-halves method, notice that only one test administration is necessary to estimate the reliability coefficient.

Table 7.5

Test Results From a High School English Test for the Calculation of the K-R 21

Name	Score
Kim	72
Donald	66
Jenny	84
Natalie	64
Cristen	72
Mary	86
Dean	82
Amie	80
Michael	80
Leeann	78
Rachael	62
Aileen	80
Becky	76
Katey	76
Amy	76
Susanne	84
Kimberly	58
Brian	80
Tony	72
William	74
	$\overline{X} = 75.100$
	$S_x = 7.718$

$$\text{K-R 21} = \left(\frac{100}{100-1}\right)\left(1 - \frac{75.10\,(100-75.10)}{100\,(59.57)}\right) = 0.693$$

Calculation 7.5

From the data displayed in Table 7.5, we can calculate an estimate of reliability by using the K-R 21 formula. In this case, our reliability coefficient is 0.693 (see Calculation 7.5). Therefore, we can conclude that because the K-R 21 reliability coefficient is above 0.60, the test results are within acceptable range for classroom use.

CHECK FOR UNDERSTANDING

7.4. What can a teacher do to maximize the reliability and validity of test results?

7.5. Calculate a split-halves reliability coefficient from the data in Table 7.6.

7.6. Based on the reliability coefficient that you calculated from the data in Table 7.6, use the Spearman-Brown formula to calculate a more accurate estimate of reliability.

Table 7.6

Music Test Scores for a Group of Seventh-Grade Students

Student	Score on odd-numbered items (x)	Score on even-numbered items (y)
Terry	6	10
Sam	8	7
Barbara	3	6
Susan	9	9
Tammy	5	7
Jim	9	6
Earl	9	8
Pete	8	9
Irene	8	7
Sally	9	7
Kelly	7	10
Arlene	8	8
Billy	7	7
Mark	8	9
Gary	9	10
Louis	6	9
Luke	8	8
William	10	9
Stacey	4	5
Herman	9	8
Gene	10	9

7.7. Using the K-R 21 method, calculate a reliability coefficient from the data displayed in Table 7.7. Assume that the test is based on a total of 50 questions, each worth 1 point. Based on the calculated reliability coefficient, is the estimated reliability within acceptable range for classroom use?

Table 7.7

Results of a Fifth-Grade Mathematics Test

Student	Score on odd-numbered items (x)
John	42
Tamba	48
Barbie	43
Susan	39
Tawnie	35
Jerry	49
Earl	39
Peter	38
Ilene	28
Sally	39
Kara	47
Arlene	38
Billy	37
Mark	38
Garrett	39
Lou	46
Laurence	38
William	50
Samantha	44
Isaac	49
George	30

7.8. Explain why we used the Spearman-Brown method when we calculated the reliability estimate with the split-halves method.

TEST SCORE ERROR

On any test, a student has a true score, a hypothetical, error-free score that could occur only if the test instrument had perfect reliability (+1.00). Realistically, most tests are not perfectly reliable, so the actual scores that students obtain on a test have a range of error. Although a student's true score is theoretical, you can estimate the range of scores surrounding the true score by using a normal equivalent.

As a concrete example of test score error, think of the score that you earned on your last test. Was the score lower or higher than you expected? If it was lower, what factors—such as lack of sleep, not enough time to complete the test, or illness—affected your score? If the test score was higher than you expected, what factors—such as extra time, a cheat sheet, or a test constructed with a high percentage of give-away items—affected your score? Given all the variables that can affect a test score, it is impossible to determine a person's true score on any test. The best that we can do is to estimate the approximate distance of the true score from the obtained score, as shown in Equation 7.3.

Equation 7.3

Obtained score = true score +/− amount of error

On any test, a true score may be higher or lower than the obtained score. As a classroom teacher, you can minimize the amount of error by maximizing the reliability of your test results. To quantify the amount of error, a statistical procedure known as the standard error of measurement is used.

The Standard Error of Measurement

Any test taker's obtained score contains a range of error that approximates the range of the true score. The *standard error of measurement* (S_m) is a statistical procedure used to estimate the amount of error in an obtained test score (see Equation 7.4). By knowing the S_m, we can estimate each test taker's true score range. For example, if a test is worth 100 points and a student scores 70 on a test with an S_m of 5, this student's score could range between 65 and 75. As a general rule for teachers, higher reliability of a test results in a lower S_m. Thus, a lower S_m signifies that a test result is closer to the true score.

The standard error of measurement gives the probability that a test score reflects the true score. To calculate the standard error of measurement, we need to know the reliability coefficient and the standard deviation of a group of scores. For example, if a test publisher reports that a K-R 21 reliability coefficient $(r_{K\text{-}R\,21})$ for a group of eighth graders is $r_{K\text{-}R\,21} = 0.87$ and the standard deviation of the test scores is 10.20, we can use the S_m formula found in Equation 7.4 to calculate the standard error of measurement (see Calculation 7.6).

Equation 7.4

$$S_m = S\sqrt{1-r}$$

Calculation 7.6

$$S_m = 10.20 \sqrt{1 - 0.87} = 3.68$$

Calculation 7.6 shows a standard error of measurement of 3.68. Recalling from our previous discussion on the normal curve, we know that about 68% or approximately 2/3 of all scores fall within one standard deviation above or below the mean (see Figure 7.1). Likewise, about 68% of all test scores fall within +/- 1 S_m (i.e., plus or minus one standard error of measurement) of the test takers' true scores. About 95% of the test scores fall within two standard errors of measurement (see Figure 7.1); therefore, we can estimate that 95% of the test scores fall within +/- 2 S_m (i.e., plus or minus two standard errors of measurement) of the test takers' true scores. Finally, if we include three standard errors of measurement, we find that about 99% of the test scores fall within +/- 3 S_m (i.e., plus or minus three standard errors of measurement) of the test takers' true scores. In this case, we are 99% confident that that the test takers' true scores fall within three standard deviations.

Using our calculated S_m of 3.68 from Calculation 7.6, if a student's score on a reading test is 75 including +/- 1 S_m, we now can estimate that there is a 68% chance that this student's true score falls between 71.32 and 78.68. Another way of looking at it is the student's true score is 75, +/- 3.68. To be more exact, there is a 95% chance that the student's true score is between 67.64 and 82.36. In this case, because we have estimated our error to cover 95% of the

Figure 7.1

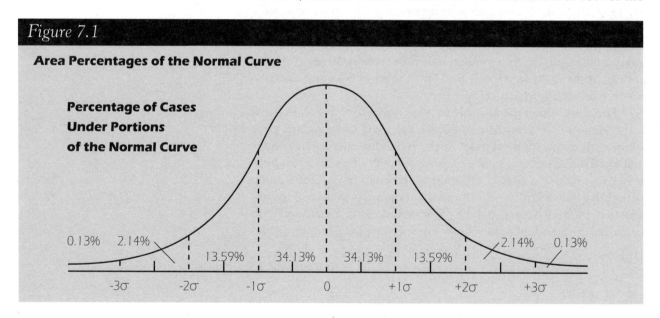

Area Percentages of the Normal Curve

Percentage of Cases Under Portions of the Normal Curve

0.13%   2.14%   13.59%   34.13%   34.13%   13.59%   2.14%   0.13%

-3σ   -2σ   -1σ   0   +1σ   +2σ   +3σ

normal curve, we multiply the S_m by 2, and estimate the range of the true score to be 75, +/- 7.36.

There is an inverse relationship between the calculated S_m and the reliability coefficient. In other words, the higher a test's reliability coefficient, the lower its S_m. As a result, low reliability coefficients indicate high measurement errors in the scores obtained on a test. Because no test is perfectly reliable, the obtained scores on a test are only estimates of a test taker's true score. Therefore, when interpreting test scores, remember that small differences in test results between test takers might not signify a true score difference. For example, the S_m on the verbal section of the SAT is 30. Therefore, if Joe scored 680 on the verbal section of the SAT and Mike scored 700, it is possible, that if the two boys took the test again, Joe could score 710 and Mike could score 670. Teachers, parents, and administrators should use extreme caution when making high-stakes decisions with test results.

CHECK FOR UNDERSTANDING

7.9.   In your own words, explain the standard error of measurement.

7.10.   Using the data in Table 7.7, calculate the standard error of measurement.

7.11.   Calculate the standard error of measurement (S_m) for a test that has a mean of 1017, a standard deviation of 209, and a reliability coefficient of 0.92.

CALCULATOR EXPLORATION

Using the TI-73, TI-83, or TI-84 graphing calculator, you can easily compute a reliability coefficient by following these key strokes.

TI-73

1.   Display list editor by pressing LIST. Here, you can enter up to 999 elements. Under L1, list all of the scores from the Test #1 that are listed in Table 7.1. Next, under L2, list all of the scores for Test #2.

2.   Press 2nd LIST to activate STAT. Next, scroll to the right and select CALC. Next, scroll down to 5: LinReg (ax+b), press 5, then press ENTER.

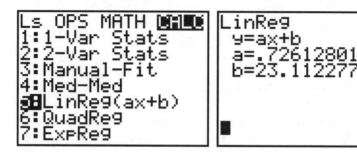

3.   Press 2nd APPS to activate VARS. Next, scroll down to 3: Statistics and press 3. Next, scroll over to EQ and scroll down to 5: r, select 5, and press ENTER. Press ENTER again to get the validity coefficient.

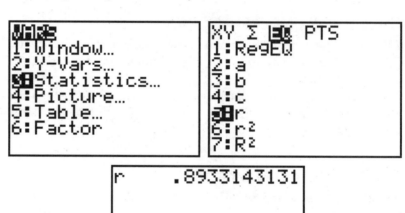

TI-83/84

1. First press STAT. Next, select 1: Edit by pressing 1. Here you can enter up to 999 elements. Under L1, list all of the scores from the Test #1 that are listed in Table 7.1. Next, under L2, list all of the scores listed under Test #2 in Table 7.1.

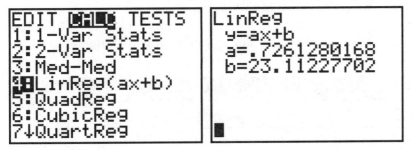

2. Press STAT and scroll to the right and select CALC. Next, scroll down to 4: LinReg (ax+b), press 4, and press ENTER.

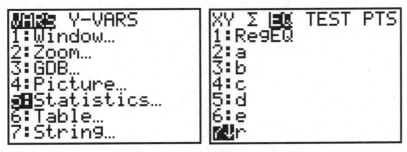

3. Press VARS. Next, scroll down to 5: Statistics and press 5. Next, scroll over to EQ. Next, scroll down to 7: r, and press 7. Press ENTER again to get the validity coefficient.

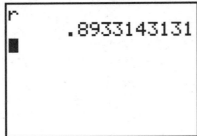

MAXIMIZING RELIABILITY

In an effort to maximize the reliability of test results, teachers should try to control factors that can decrease reliability. Table 7.8 presents a list of factors that can increase variance, and thus decrease reliability, of test scores.

IN SUMMARY

The reliability of test results is based on the calculation of a reliability coefficient that measures the consistency of the students' scores. To maximize reliability during test administration, a teacher should adhere to the principles of test administration and construction presented throughout this textbook and be aware of the variables of the Test Reliabity Checklist in Table 7.8.

Several different methods are used to calculate reliability coefficients. The test-retest method of estimating reliability is computed when the same group of students takes the same test on two different test administrations. The alternate forms method uses two different tests with equivalent items. The split-halves method estimates reliability when the individual items of the test

Table 7.8

Test Reliability Checklist

Test Administration Variables	(√) If satisfactory
1. Health, fatigue, and emotional strain of the students	
2. Motivation and rapport with the examiner	
3. Effects of heat, light, noise, and ventilation	
4. Level of practice on skills required by tests of this type	
5. Changes in fatigue or motivation developed by the test instrument (e.g., discouragement resulting from failure on a particular item)	
6. Fluctuations in attention, coordination, or standards of judgment	
7. Fluctuations in memory for particular facts	
8. Level of practice on skills or knowledge required by this particular test (e.g., effects of special coaching)	
9. Temporary emotional states and strengths of habits, related to particular test stimuli (e.g., a question calls to mind a recent bad dream)	
10. Luck in the selection of answers by guessing	

* Adapted from: 1. Thorndike, R.L. 1949. *Personnel selection.* New York: Wiley; 2. Cronbach, L.J. 1970. *Essentials of psychological testing.* New York: Harper Publishing.

are examined internally. The split-halves method has two steps: dividing the test into two subtests and calculating a Spearman-Brown correlation coefficient to estimate reliability. Finally, the Kuder-Richardson method estimates a reliability coefficient from a single test administration.

After the reliability coefficient is calculated, the standard error of measurement (S_m) is determined to estimate the range of the true score. The standard error of measurement (S_m) is a statistical procedure that is used to estimate the amount of error in an obtained test score.

CHAPTER REVIEW QUESTIONS

7.12. From the data in Table 7.9, calculate a split-halves reliability coefficient with the Spearman-Brown formula to correct for the error caused by splitting the test in half.

Table 7.9

Trigonometry Test Results

Student	Score on odd-numbered items (x)	Score on even-numbered items (y)
1	9	9
2	8	7
3	8	6
4	9	10
5	5	7
6	4	6
7	9	4
8	7	9
9	8	7
10	9	7
11	8	8
12	8	8
13	7	10
14	8	7
15	9	8
16	6	10
17	9	8
18	10	10
19	9	5
20	9	8

7.13. From the data below in Table 7.10, calculate an alternate forms reliability coefficient for two administrations of the same biology test. Based on the reliability coefficient that was calculated from the data presented in Table 7.10, is the test acceptable for classroom use? Please explain your answer.

Table 7.10

Equivalent Forms of a 10th-Grade Biology Test

Student	Biology Test Day #1	Biology Test Day #3
1	97	91
2	67	72
3	66	67
4	99	87
5	83	88
6	74	78
7	100	90
8	84	78
9	83	87
10	79	79

7.14. Which of the following reliability coefficients would be the most useful for a classroom teacher? Explain your answer.
a. 0.33
b. 0.59
c. 0.82
d. 1.10

7.15. Of the three tests in Table 7.11, which test has the highest S_m? Which test's results show the lowest level of consistency? Explain your answer.

Table 7.11

Results of Three Classroom Tests

Test	Mean	SD	Reliability Coefficient
#1	85	15	0.61
#2	82	8	0.79
#3	78	7	0.81

7.16.   Calculate the standard error of measurement (S_m) for a test that has a mean of 70, a standard deviation of 10, and a reliability coefficient of 0.610.

7.17.   Based on your standard error of measurement calculation from question 7.16, calculate the range of scores showing a 68% chance that the scores fall within 1 S_m. Next, calculate the range of scores showing a 95% chance that the scores fall within 2 S_m.

7.18.   List some possible reasons why errors occur with test results. As a teacher, what can you do to minimize test error?

7.19.   Explain how each of the following types of reliability is calculated:
a. Test-retest
b. Alternate forms
c. K-R 21

7.20.   List several factors that affect the reliability of test results. See Table 7.8, p. 156, for possible answers.

7.21.   Use the following set of data to determine the mean, median, mode, range, variance, standard deviation, standard error of measurement, and possible range for each score assuming 68% confidence. The reliability coefficient is 0.85.

Data: 100, 95, 51, 77, 65, 81, 90, 92, 76, 76, 74, 88
Mean: _____
Median: _____
Mode: _____
Range: _____
Variance: _____
Standard deviation: _____
Standard error of measurement: _____

Obtained Score	Range From	To	Obtained score	Range From	To
100	_____	_____	90	_____	_____
95	_____	_____	92	_____	_____
51	_____	_____	76	_____	_____
77	_____	_____	76	_____	_____
65	_____	_____	74	_____	_____
81	_____	_____	88	_____	_____

Interpreting Assessment Data

ANSWERS: CHECK FOR UNDERSTANDING

7.1.   Yes, the results can be consistent; however, they are not on target.

7.2.   -1.0 to +1.0

7.3.   Reliability is the consistency of the results and validity is the extent to which a test measures what it claims to measure.

7.4.   Teachers should try to control factors that can decrease reliability (see Table 7.8).

7.5.   The reliability coefficient is (r) = 0.413.

7.6.   R = 0.585

7.7.   Kuder-Richardson 21 reliability coefficient is r = 0.809, which is in an acceptable range for classroom use.

7.8.   The Spearman Brown gives a better estimate of the reliability coefficient when using the split-halves method.

7.9.   The standard error of measurement (S_m) is a statistical procedure used to estimate the amount of error in an obtained test score.

7.10. The calculation is based on the K-R 21 r = 0.809, with a standard deviation of S = 6.024. Thus, the standard error of measurement is 2.6 for this test.

7.11. The standard error of measurement is 59.11.

ANSWERS: CHAPTER REVIEW QUESTIONS

7.12. The reliability correlation coefficient (r) = 0.056. The Spearman–Brown correction is R = 0.106.

7.13. The reliability coefficient is (r) = 0.883. The test is acceptable for classroom use because the reliablity coefficient of 0.883 exceeds 0.60, the base rate for predictive validity according to Taylor and Russell (1939).

7.14. c. 0.82. The reliability coefficient of 0.82 is the only acceptable coefficient among the possible answers because it exceeds 0.60, the base rate for predictive validity according to Taylor and Russell (1939).

7.15. The lowest consistency is Test #1, which reports a reliability coefficient of 0.61. The test with the highest standard error is Test #1 as well, which results from a lower reliability and a higher standard deviation.

7.16. 6.24.

7.17. $1 S_m$ = 63.76 to 76.24
       $2 S_m$ = 57.52 to 82.48

7.18. Standard error can occur with test results when there is high variability and low reliability. Teachers can minimize standard error by using the Test Reliability Checklist in Table 7.8.

7.19.   The test-retest and the alternate forms use the Pearson Correlation formula. The Kuder Richardson uses the following:

$$K\text{-}R\ 21 = \left(\frac{K}{K-1}\right)\left(1 - \frac{M\,(K-M)}{K*s^2}\right)$$

7.20.   See Table 7.8, p. 156, for possible answers.

7.21.   Mean: 80.42
         Median: 79
         Mode: 76
         Range: 49
         Variance: 188.5
         Standard deviation: 13.73
         Standard error of measurement: 5.32

Obtained score	Range From	To	Obtained score	Range From	To
100	94.68	105.32	90	84.68	95.32
95	89.68	100.32	92	86.68	97.32
51	45.68	56.32	76	70.68	81.32
77	71.68	82.32	76	70.68	81.32
65	59.68	70.32	74	68.68	79.32
81	75.68	86.32	88	82.68	93.32

INTERNET RESOURCES

www.statsoftinc.com/textbook/streliab.html

The StatSoft Inc. website gives a general introduction and advanced overview on the concept of reliability. This site serves students who are looking for information on reliability that goes beyond the scope of the discussion in this textbook.

www.education-world.com/a_issues/issues096.shtml

The Education World website continues its series on high-stakes testing today. What do the experts, national teacher organizations, and presidential candidates have to say about these tests?

www.ncme.org

The website of the National Council of Measurement in Education offers links and other sources related to the concept of reliability.

REFERENCES

Cronbach, L. J. 1970. *Essentials of psychological testing.* New York: Harper Publishing.

Richardson, M. W., and G. F. Kuder. 1939. The calculation of test reliability coefficients based upon the method of rational equivalence. *Journal of Educational Psychology* 30: 681–687.

Taylor, H. C., and J. T. Russell. 1939. The relationship of validity coefficients to the practical effectiveness of tests in selection: Discussion and tables. *Journal of Applied Psychology* 23: 565–578.

Thorndike, R. L. 1949. *Personnel selection.* New York: Wiley.

FURTHER READING

Allen, M. J., and W. M. Yen. 1979. *Introduction to measurement theory.* Prospect Heights, IL: Waveland.

American Educational Research Association (AERA), American Psychological Association (APA), and National Council on Measurement in Education (NCME). 1999. *Standards for educational and psychological testing, 3rd ed.* Washington, DC: AERA.

Christmann, E. P., and J. L. Badgett. 2000. A four-year analytic comparison of eleventh grade academic achievement in the Slippery Rock Area High School, and district pupil expenditures. Research report presented to The Slippery Rock School District's Board of Directors and The Pennsylvania Department of Education. (ERIC Document No. ED443824)

Cronbach, L. J., and P. Meehl. 1955. Construct validity in psychological tests. *Psychological Bulletin* 52: 281–302.

Elmore, P. B., and P. L. Woehlke. 1997. *Basic statistics.* New York: Longman.

Gravetter, F. J., and L. B. Wallnau. 2002. *Essentials of statistics for the behavioral sciences.* New York: West.

Raymondu, J. C. 1999. *Statistical analysis in the behavioral sciences.* New York: McGraw-Hill.

Richardson, M. W., and F. Kuder. 1939. The calculation of test reliability coefficients based upon the method of rational equivalence. *Journal of Educational Psychology* 30: 681–687.

Thorndike, R. L., and E. P. Hagen. 1978. *The cognitive abilities test.* Lombard, IL: Riverside.

Thorne, B. M., and J. M. Giesen. 2000. *Statistics for the behavioral sciences.* Mountain View, CA: Mayfield.

Zawojewski, J. S., and J. M. Shaughnessy. 2000. Mean and median: Are they really so easy? *Mathematics Teaching in the Middle School* 5 (7): 436–440.

OTHER RESOURCES

Anastasi, A. 1988. *Psychological testing, 6th ed.* New York: MacMillan.

Angoff, W. H. 1984. *Scales, norms, and equivalent scores.* Princeton, NJ: Educational Testing Service.

Bennett, R., and W. Ward. 1993. *Construction versus choice in cognitive measurement.* Hillsdale, NJ: Lawrence Erlbaum.

Berk, R. A., ed. 1980. *Criterion-referenced measurement: The state of the art.* Baltimore: Johns Hopkins University Press.

Coombs, C. H. 1964. *A theory of data.* New York: Wiley.

Crocker, L., and J. Algina. 1986. *Introduction to classical and modern test theory.* New York: Holt, Rinehart, and Winston.

Cronbach, L. J. 1990. *The essentials of psychological testing, 5th ed.* New York: Harper and Row.

Cronbach, L. J., G. C. Gleser, H. Nanda, and N. Rajaratnam. 1972. *The dependability of behavioral measurements.* New York: Wiley.

Council of Chief State School Officers. 1992. Recommendations for improving the assessment and monitoring of students with limited English proficiency. Washington, DC: Author.

Davison, M. L. 1983. *Multidimensional scaling.* New York: Wiley.

Gorsuch, R. L. 1983. *Factor analysis.* Hillsdale, NJ: Lawrence Erlbaum.

Guilford, J. P. 1954. *Psychometric methods.* New York: McGraw-Hill.

Gulliksen, H. 1950. *Theory of mental tests.* New York: Wiley.

Haladyna, T. M. 1994. Developing and validating multiple-choice test items. Hillsdale, NJ: Lawrence Erlbaum.

Hambleton, R. K., and H. Swaminathan. 1985. *Item response theory.* Boston: Kluwer-Nijoff.

Hambleton, R. K., H. Swaminathan, and L. Rogers. 1991. *Fundamentals of item response theory.* Newbury Park, CA: Sage.

Holland, P. W., and D. B. Rubin. 1982. *Test equating.* New York: Academic Press.

Holland, P. W., and H. Wainer, eds. 1993. *Differential item functioning.* Hillsdale, NJ: Lawrence Erlbaum.

Joint Committee on Testing Practices. 1988. *Code of fair testing practices in education.* Washington, DC: American Psychological Association.

Lindquist, E. F., ed. 1951. *Educational measurement.* Washington, DC: American Council on Education.

Linn, R., ed. *Educational measurement, 3rd ed.* Washington, DC: American Council on Education.

Lord, F. M. 1980. *Applications of item response theory to practical testing problems.* Hillsdale, NJ: Lawrence Erlbaum.

Lord, F. M., and M. R. Novick. 1968. *Statistical theories of mental test scores.* Reading, MA: Addison-Wesley.

Luce, R. D. 1959. *Individual choice behavior.* New York: Wiley.

Nunnally, J. C., and I. H. Bernstein. 1994. *Psychometric theory.* New York: McGraw-Hill.

Shavelson, R .J., and N. M. Webb. 1991. *Generalizability theory: A primer.* Newbury Park, CA: Sage.

Stevens, S. S. 1951. *Mathematics, measurement, and psychophysics.* In S. S. Stevens, ed., *Handbook of experimental psychology.* New York: Wiley.

Taylor, H. C., and J. T. Russell. 1939. The relationship of validity coefficients to the practical effectiveness of tests in selection: Discussion and tables. *Journal of Applied Psychology* 23: 565–578.

Thorndike, R. L., ed. 1971. *Educational measurement, 2nd ed.* Washington, DC: American Council on Education.

Torgerson, W. S. 1958. *Theory and methods of scaling.* New York: Wiley.

Traub, R. E. 1994. *Reliability for the social sciences: Theory and applications.* Newbury Park, CA: Sage.

Wainer, H., and H. I. Braun. 1988. *Test validity.* Hillsdale, NJ: Lawrence Erlbaum.

Willingham, W. W., M. Ragosta, R. E. Bennett, H. Braun, D. A. Rock, and D. E. Powers, eds. 1988. *Testing handicapped people.* Needham Heights, MA: Allyn and Bacon.

Chapter 8

GRADING

OBJECTIVES

When you complete this chapter, you should be able to
1. compare and contrast different types of grading systems,
2. calculate classroom grades,
3. use a record book for organizing grades,
4. apply computer applications to grading, and
5. report academic achievement to parents and students.

Key Terms

When you complete this chapter, you should be able to understand

differential grading   pass/fail grade system
electronic grade book   percentage-grade system
grade inflation   record book
grades   report card
letter-grade system

Many criticisms have been launched against grades in general because of their perceived failure to portray student achievement accurately. In many instances, these criticisms are just. But, if student grades are reflections of measurable instructional objectives, which are the basis of objective assessment, then they can accurately represent student achievement.

As we have emphasized throughout previous chapters, well-defined objectives are the foundations of virtually all methods of objective assessment. Such objectives make for measurable means of assessment because they provide the framework for the assessment. For example, a performance-based objective that is specific in its student requirements provides guidelines for the construction of a quantitative rubric. Moreover, quantitative assessment reduces the opportunities for grading subjectivity.

Student grades should not be based on any single method of assessment. Rather, they should result from a variety of assessments. For example, students' portfolios should serve as a vehicle of explanation for both student and parents, because a meaningful portfolio will contain representative samples of all of a student's

work within each of the cognitive and academic levels. In addition, both parents and the student will recognize any grade as more credible if the components of the portfolio are selected and entered by the student and his or her teacher.

Your students and their parents will more readily accept grades if these grades have a quantitative baseline. As assurance of this quantitative baseline, virtually every component that is factored into the grade should also have a quantitative baseline, whether it is a test, a project, a performance, a paper, a demonstration, or any other assignment. As previous chapters have pointed out, however, these baselines should be legitimately quantitative, because the simple assignment of numbers to subjective judgments is often an act of deception. For example, if a numerical score is awarded to an essay test, paper, or a project in the absence of a clearly defined and quantitative rubric, the assigned score becomes a misrepresentation.

Just as your tests should have content validity, so should your grades. That is, your tests should be representative samples of the material that you have taught, and they should be weighted according to the importance of this material. For example, the more important the material, the greater the number of items pertaining to this material should be included in the test. The same is true of your grades: The more important the assessed assignment, the more heavily it should be weighted into the grade.

Grades should be representations of students' academic achievement. They should reflect only academic performance: not attitudes or social behavior. Should you wish to report attitudes or social behavior, you should use standard forms furnished by your school district, or you could refer to appropriate portfolio reflections entered by you and your students. Regardless of what you report, you should be able to support your statements with observable data.

Our primary purpose as teachers is to enhance the learning of our students. Acknowledging this, we also understand that students learn best when they are motivated. With this in mind, we would do well to consider grades as a motivational force because they can serve both as long-term goals and as rewards. Furthermore, your daily assignments, the means to composite grades, can serve as more immediate goals and rewards for your students. Grades can be not only accurate representations of your pupils' achievement but sources of motivation as well.

Over the years ways in which students' grades are reported have expanded. Your school district will provide you with a policy manual that explains the district's grading system. You should adhere to the district's policy when reporting grades. Most teachers, however, have choices when it comes to reporting grades for their individual classes. The remainder of this chapter will explain the fundamentals of grading systems and the procedures for computing and reporting grades.

GRADING SYSTEMS

Letter Grades

Letter grades, the most common system of grading in use today, usually appear in a sequence of A, B, C, D, and F, with an "A" representing excellent achievement, a "B" representing above-average achievement, a "C" representing average achievement, a "D" representing below-average achievement, and an "F" representing failure. Based on predetermined criteria, the letter-grade system provides a summary of academic achievement as a single grade. Some school districts have modified grading systems with alternatives such as numbers (1, 2, 3, 4, and 5) or use letters such as "O" for outstanding, "S" for satisfactory, and "U" for unsatisfactory.

Although letter grades are designed to report students' academic achievement, this system (A, B, C, D, F) has become so common that people now use it to rate everyday things such as movies, restaurants, and sporting events. Moreover, this system is easily converted into grade-point averages by equating letter grades with numbers: A = 4, B = 3, C = 2, D = 1; and these grade point averages (e.g., 3.25) can be used by college admissions personnel and by prospective employees. Yet, even though letter grades may be the standard for grading throughout American schools, a disadvantage lies in the wide range of a single letter grade. For example a student who earns a low "B" average cannot be distinguished from a student who earns a high "B" average because both grades are in the same category. Subsequently, some school systems have adopted a plus-minus system, in which the high "B" student gets a grade of a "B+" and the low "B" student earns a grade of "B-." The plus-minus system can be designed to show different variations within categories (see Table 8.1).

Table 8.1

Examples of +/- Systems of Grading

Grade	Grade Points		Percentage	Grade
A	4.000		93–100%	A
A-	3.700		90–92%	A-
B+	3.300		87–89%	B+
B	3.000		83–86%	B
B-	2.700		80–82%	B-
C+	2.300		77–79%	C+
C	2.000		73–76%	C
C-	1.700		70–72%	C-
D	1.000		60–69%	D
F	0.000		Below 60%	F

Percentage Grades

Using a percentage of 100, percentage grades are based on the percentage of correct items or total points earned on a test or assignment. For example, if there is a maximum of 50 points on a test and a student earns a 44, the percentage grade is an 88%. This is determined by taking the total of earned points divided by the total points on the test, which results in a proportion of 0.88. Next, to calculate a percentage, multiply the proportion by 100, resulting in a percentage of 88%. The advantage of this type of grading system is that it shows the variation between high and low scores. In some school districts, the percentage grading system is used for both marking period grades and final course grades. Most report cards, however, have grading scales so that the percentage grade can be categorized as a letter grade (see Table 8.2).

Table 8.2

Letter Grade and Percentage Equivalents

Letter Grade	Percentage Equivalent
A	90% to 100%
B	80% to 89%
C	70% to 79%
D	60% to 69%
F	Below 60%

Some school districts use higher percentages for a given letter grade than those shown in Table 8.2. For example, some schools require a minimum of 93% for an "A." Our position is that the grades should be valid and reliable. Adjusting a grading scale to decrease grade inflation is merely treating the symptoms of a much larger problem.

Another issue that arises with percentage grades occurs when a student finishes the marking period with an average that the percentage scale shown in Table 8.2 is not designed to resolve. For example, what if a student finishes the marking period with an 89.5% average? The student might ask, "Is an 89.5% an "A" or a "B?" It is better to be proactive rather than reactive. One possible solution is to accompany your percentage grading system with a point system such as the one depicted in Table 8.3.

Table 8.3

Point System

Letter Grade	Points Needed
A	270 points to 300 points (90% to 100%)
B	240 points to 269 points (80% to 89.67%)
C	210 points to 239 points (70% to 79.66%)
D	180 points to 209 points (60% to 69.67%)
F	Below 180 points (Below 60%)

As you can see, this system lets the students know exactly what is expected to earn one of the five letter grades.

Pass/Fail Grades

Pass/fail grades result in a final grade of either pass (P) or fail (F). One of the benefits of this system is that it can reduce some of the anxieties related to taking certain high school or college courses. For example, a college student who is apprehensive about taking chemistry and is not required to do so might elect to take it voluntarily if he or she is given the option to take the course pass/fail. The advantage here is that, if the student earns a pass, perhaps only a "C" under the traditional system, the student's grade point average could not be pulled down. Unfortunately, the pass/fail grading system does not bolster motivation very well, because many students who elect to take courses pass/fail just do enough to get through the course. Pass/fail grades seem to work best with noncredit offerings.

CHECK FOR UNDERSTANDING

8.1.   What are the different types of grading systems?

8.2.   What is the percentage grade if a student correctly answers 36 questions out of a possible 50 questions, each worth one point, on a social studies test?

8.3.   Describe an advantage of using a percentage grading system instead of a letter grading system.

8.4.   As a student, would you prefer a letter grading system with a +/- grading system or without a +/- grading system? Please explain the rationale for your preference.

Calculating and Recording Classroom Grades

After you have created a test and administered it, the next step is to grade it. As a general rule, try to return the test results to the students as soon as possible. Homework should be returned within one day and comprehensive exams within one week. Formative assessments such as homework, lab reports, and worksheets can be returned to the students and taken home. You should exercise a high degree of test security with all hour-long and final examinations. Allowing students to take an examination outside of the classroom is not advisable. If you choose to review the exam with the entire class, have the students clear all materials from their desks and review the exam in an orderly manner. Remember, an examination is designed to measure academic achievement. Summative examinations should not be designed as learning instruments per se. In any case, you should give your students the opportunity to debrief. So that instructional time is not wasted, you should debrief before or after school or during noninstructional time during school, such as a study hall, so that course instruction can be maximized.

Throughout the school year, you should keep a record of students' grades. Depending on your school district's policy, each marking period use the recorded grades to calculate a final report card grade, which will be averaged into a final grade for the year. The grades will consist of the ongoing formative assessments—such as homework, classwork, and quizzes—along with the summative assessments—such as unit exams, final exams, and book reports—you have administered throughout the marking period. As a general rule, you should use formative assessments on a daily basis. That way, both you and your students will get the valuable feedback needed to make the necessary adjustments to improve teaching and learning. Summative assessments should be administered after all of the learning objectives have been covered through labs, lectures, homework, cooperative learning activities, and other such means. As a result, academic achievement will have been established and recorded in a class record book. Class record books are available in a variety of formats.

Most class record books are arranged in columns and rows, where the first column represents the students' name and the subsequent columns provide space to record daily grades, attendance, participation, and whatever else you may wish. Most record books have 50 spaces (5 days in a week and 10 weeks in a marking period) for recording daily grades and documenting classroom management. You could, for example, document students who are late or absent from class. In addition, there is usually space in the right-hand column to average the daily grades with the summative grades.

Computer Applications in Grading

Another possibility for keeping track of classroom grades is a spreadsheet, which can be used to store data and compute final course grades. A kaleidoscope of websites is available that show you how to put together your own spreadsheets for calculating grades (see list of websites at the end of this chapter). The advantage of a spreadsheet is that it can be programmed to factor in different grading systems. A spreadsheet consists of a grid of rows and columns, called cells, that enables you to organize data in a readily understandable format. The data are connected through a built-in calculator: If you change the number in one cell, all of the cells that are dependent on that cell change automatically. Figure 8.1 is a sample of a spreadsheet used as a class record book.

Figure 8.1

Sample of a Spreadsheet

Mr. Smith's Science Class									
Name	Test 1	Test 2	Test 3	Homework	Project	Absent	Labs	Final Exam	Final Grade
Biando, Sue	97.0	100.0	91.0	90.0	95.0	1.0	91.0	88.0	93.0
Ferguson, Jane	85.0	81.0	97.0	99.0	93.0	2.0	89.0	87.0	90.1
Heupel, William	80.0	82.0	84.0	99.0	90.0	1.0	90.0	99.0	89.1
Marks, Donna	78.0	99.0	94.0	87.0	83.0	5.0	100.0	78.0	88.4
Santaserio, Cleo	80.0	92.0	81.0	89.0	78.0	3.0	72.0	84.0	82.3
Thomson, Avery	75.0	84.0	73.0	84.0	79.0	2.0	83.0	70.0	78.3
Class Average	82.5	89.7	86.3	91.3	86.3	2.3	87.5	84.3	86.9

Electronic Grade Books

Several different computerized technologies are available for classroom testing and measurement applications. The current electronic grade book programs are a valuable innovation for classroom teachers (see Figure 8.2 for a comprehensive listing of available packages). Electronic grade books enable you to enter student names, generate seating charts, and organize class records, such as grades, absences, and discipline problems. In addition, grade book software packages calculate grades and generate reports.

Figure 8.2

Grade Book Software Packages

1st Class Software—1st Class GradeBook *[www.1stclasssoftware. com/default.asp]*

CalEd Software—Class Action Gradebook *[www. classactiongradebook.com]*

Calico Educational Software—FastTracker *[www.softpile.com/ authors/Calico_Educational_Software_Inc_.html]*

CampusWare—GradeSpeed *[www.gradespeed.net/Campusware/ gs/index.htm]*

Chariot Software—MicroGrade *[www.chariot.com/micrograde/ index.asp]*

Class Mate Software—Class Mate Grading Software *[www. classmategrading.com]*

ClassBuilder Software—ClassBuilder *[www.classbuilder.com]*

Common Goal Systems—TeacherEase *[www.teacherease.com]*

E-Z Grader—E-Z Grader [www.ezgrader.com]

EdSoft Software—Instructional Management System *[www.ed-soft. com]*

eSembler—eSembler for Education *[www.esembler.com]*

Excelsior Software—Pinnacle [www.excelsiorsoftware.com]

Jackson Software—GradeQuick *[www.jacksonsoftware.com]*

Misty City Software—Grade Machine *[www.mistycity.com]*

Differential Grading

You should also be aware of the differential grading options available for reporting the progress of your special-needs students.

You may wish, for instance, to list the student's actual grade level followed by a listing of the particular content grade level at which the student is performing and concluding with the letter grade earned by the student within his or her respective performance level.

Judy: Grade 4
Mathematics Level: Grade 3
Grade Level Performance: B

As another option, you may decide to cite the student's actual grade level; list the grade level at which he is performing in a particular academic area; but report his work behaviors as opposed to his skill level.

Sammy: Grade 4
Mathematics Level: Grade 3
Works Independently: B
Completed Assignments: B+
Neatness: B

Another possibility is to state the student's individual education plan goals, formulated by you, his parents, and professional staff members, and then indicate which of these goals have been met and which still require work.

"By the end of the first grading period, Ishmail will solve computational problems at the 3.5 grade level."
Ishmail: Grade 5
Mathematics Level: Grade 3
Goal: Met

You could possibly decide to replace letter grades with pass/fail or with satisfactory/needs improvement.

Sherri: Grade 4
Reading Level: Grade 2
Reading Level Performance: Pass

You could also decide to assign more than one grade in a single area.

Elo: Grade 4
Reading Level: Grade 4
Reading Achievement: B
Effort: C

PREVENTING CHEATING

According to Callahan (2004), 74% of high school students have admitted to cheating at some point during school. Because of this documented problem, you must be vigilant in prohibiting students from any breach of academic integrity. The plagiarism of written assignments and cheating on tests compromises the validity and reliability of the results. Some examples of cheating that you may encounter in your classroom are

1. unauthorized use of calculators, graphing calculators, PDAs, cellular phones, and electronic devices;
2. discussing the content of a test, quiz, or homework assessment with students who have not begun the assessment;
3. sharing student work that should be done independently;
4. using crib notes during test situations;
5. submitting work that has been presented previously by another student; and
6. obtaining test or quiz materials before assessment without the instructor's knowledge.

Rather than reacting to these situations, which sometimes may be necessary, we propose a proactive approach. For example, when using multiple-choice tests, have more than one written version of the test with a different item-response pattern randomly distributed among the students. With this approach, students may be discouraged from looking at the work of others during the exam. Concurrently, you should always monitor the class during the examination. Make sure that the students are aware that you are watching them, and confront wandering eyes. Below are some helpful suggestions to minimize cheating:

1. Make students aware of both the school's policy on cheating and your classroom policy before the test's administration.
2. Have all tests and forms numbered and accounted for before and after the examination.
3. Monitor the students during the examination. Never leave the classroom without arranging proper supervision for the students.
4. Watch for the use of crib sheets or other unauthorized materials being used by students during the examinations.
5. When using essay exams or questions, distribute blue books or special paper so that you can keep close track of materials before and after the examination.

6. If possible, make sure that students who leave the classroom during an examination for such necessities as the restroom or a nurse are supervised. That way, they will be unable to come in contact with other students or retrieve materials from lockers or other places.

7. Do not make unreasonable threats to students as a consequence of cheating. Simply follow your classroom policy, which should be based on the school district policy. For example, if you observe a student using a crib sheet, ask the student to hand it over—gather as much evidence as possible. If the student refuses to cooperate, you should turn the matter over to the principal. Keep in mind that you are not authorized to search students.

8. Before you accuse a student of cheating, gather as much evidence as possible, such as physical evidence and names of witnesses. Then follow your school policy on cheating.

DEALING WITH MISSED TESTS AND ASSIGNMENTS

It is essential that you have a policy for missing or late work. If an assignment is due at the beginning of first period, for example, and a student submits it at the beginning of seventh period, what are the consequences of the late submission? You should have a written classroom policy statement specifying the consequences of missed or late work. Below is an example of a policy for work submitted late.

Late Work Policy

For every class period that an assignment is late, 5% of the assignment's final grade will be deducted. After being late for five school days, the assignment will not be accepted. If extenuating circumstances prevent you from submitting an assignment on time, please make every attempt to communicate this before the assignment's due date so that arrangements can be made to submit the assignment without penalty.

The notion of penalizing the students for not submitting assignments on time is to deter late work. Otherwise, classroom management would be extremely chaotic.

Another issue that you might encounter is work missed due to an absence caused by an illness. Often, illnesses are unforeseen and can prevent students from attending school. You should have a plan in place to handle this type of problem. First, based on the school's policy, make sure that the student's absence is excused. If the absence is excused, you should give the student the opportunity to submit the assignment when the student has returned to school from the absence. Below is a sample of a policy for make-up work.

Make-Up Work Policy

It is the student's/parents' responsibility to have any missed work picked up when he or she is absent from school. Any missed assignments must be submitted two days after the student has returned to school from the excused illness. For example, if a child is absent on a Tuesday and returns to school on Wednesday, the student must submit the missed work on Thursday. If the work is not submitted on Thursday, it will be graded in accordance with the Late Work Policy.

There are several issues you should consider for a missed examination. However, the most important issue to consider is whether the student has a legitimate excuse for missing the test. For example, a written excuse from a licensed medical doctor, a letter from a court of law, or a death notice provides acceptable documentation for an excused absence. You should make students aware of your policy during the first class meeting. Below is an example of a class policy for a missed test.

Missed Test Policy

It is the responsibility of the student to arrange to make up a missed test on the day of returning to school. For the exam to be made up, however, the absence must be excused. Understand that a make-up exam is different from the exam given during the assigned testing session. If the student does not arrange to make up an examination or does not have an excused absence from a test, you should record a grade of zero as the test score.

Having students submit work and take exams on time is a prerequisite for optimum classroom management. Moreover, having students submit assignments on time increases the reliability and validity of grades by minimizing cheating. When a student is absent from a test or assignment, that student gains additional time to complete assignments and additional preparation time for an examination. Having students submit work on time helps them to be more responsible, which is necessary for their success in postsecondary education and when they enter the workforce.

REPORTING GRADES

We cannot overemphasize the necessity of understanding how to report grades. First, you must always grade according to your school district's grading policy. Furthermore, a report card grade should be a composite of all of the recorded grades throughout the marking period from items such as papers, projects, quizzes, laboratories, and examinations. As previously mentioned, frequent formative assessments provide the necessary feedback for students' maximum performance on summative assessments. Remember that keeping accurate records is essential for the reporting of student achievement.

In addition to students, school administrators and parents also factor into the grading process. When a grading question arises, check with a veteran teacher or administrator in your school for suggestions. Here are some suggestions that will assist you in maintaining accurate grading records.

Electronic and Traditional Teacher Record Books

If you are keeping grades in an electronic grade book, make sure that you preserve your records on a disk and always keep an up-to-date hard copy of all records at home. In addition, keep your computer in a secure location and make sure that the computer is password protected.

Traditional Teacher Record Books

Keep your record book with you at all times. Leaving it in your classroom unattended could result in its being stolen or a student's tampering with it. Always keep your record book in a secure location. Also, if at all possible, always take your record book with you during a fire drill.

Use Percentage Grading (100%)

It is best to convert all grades and numbers to a percentage grading system. This makes it easier to calculate grades and easier for your students to understand their grades.

Report Card Comments

When reporting areas of weakness, always be objective and report things that can be documented. Parents can misconstrue subjective comments, leading to unnecessary repercussions for you and your students. For example, you should not report that "Susan does not do her lab reports." Rather, you should report that "Susan did not submit laboratory reports on 9/14, 9/21, 10/7, and 11/1 during the grading period."

Report Cards

Every school district adopts a report card for reporting grades. The report card often has a grading scale, different subjects, and attendance.

CHECK FOR UNDERSTANDING

8.5.   Develop a grading system for a formative assessment that will be used with a sixth-grade mathematics course, such as a homework assignment, a classroom assignment, or a daily quiz. Include any information, such as objectives or a rubric, that will maximize the validity and reliability of the assessment.

8.6.   Develop a grading system for a summative assessment that will be used with an eighth-grade social studies course. Base your grading system on an objective test consisting of true-false and multiple-choice items. Keep in mind the number of objective items necessary for acceptable reliability. Also, remember that multiple-choice items are more conducive to the measurement of higher-level thinking skills than are true-false items.

8.7.   Using the internet, research and evaluate some of the grade book software packages listed in Figure 8.2. Evaluate the grade book software in terms of ease of use and classroom grading and management applications.

8.8.   Give an example of a situation in which you would use differential grading. In detail, describe the course, its objectives, and the students involved in the scenario.

8.9.   Write a statement designed to discourage cheating that would be read in the presence of your students before an examination. Include all rules, all instructions, and the penalty for not adhering to your policy.

8.10.   Write a missed-test policy for your course. This policy should be distributed to your students on the first day of class.

8.11.   Develop a grading system for a 36-week course. Include a variety of formative and summative assessments, the results of which will be averaged into nine-week, midterm, and final course grades.

IN SUMMARY

Like a test with high content validity, your students' grades should be representative samples of their achievement. These grades should reflect the objective assessment that results from measurable objectives. Remember also that your students' grades should be indicators of their academic achievement, not their attitudes or social behavior. This does not mean that student attitudes and behaviors should not be reported, only that you should not factor them into the students' academic grades. There are a number of ways available for reporting pupil progress. Specifically, you can opt for letter grades, percentage grades, pass/fail grades, differential grading, or combinations of these options. There are also a variety of electronic and computer sources that you can use for determining your students' grades. As a general rule, base your grading policies on those of your school district. That way, you will be more likely to establish an objective and fair system of grading for all students.

CHAPTER REVIEW QUESTIONS

8.12.   Develop a grading system for a sixth-grade mathematics class. Present this system in such a way that students, parents, and school administrators will understand how the final course grade will be earned over 36 weeks.

8.13.   You are a social studies teacher who must calculate marking-period grades. During the marking period, you administered 2 tests, 3 written papers, and 25 homework assignments. Based on the different proportion of assessments, develop a system to calculate the final marking-period grades. Include maximum points for each.

8.14.   Based on the assessment data reported below in Table 8.4, design a spreadsheet to calculate grades for the students. Base your grading system on a 10-percentage point system.

Table 8.4

Classroom Grading Sample

Student	Test #1	Test #2	Homework	Project
James	78	74	82	67
Peter	98	87	91	88
Mary	100	100	100	100
Andrew	67	77	81	89
Hannah	71	82	87	92

8.15. Based on the grades reported in Table 8.4 and using a spreadsheet, calculate the descriptive statistics (mean, median, and standard deviation) for all of the students' grades on Test #1 and Test #2. Which test had the highest mean? Which test had the highest standard deviation?

8.16. Create a syllabus for a course that you will be teaching. Include a grading system, a missed test policy, a late work policy, and a make-up work policy.

8.17. Write a class policy on cheating that will be sent home and signed by parents and returned to you at school.

8.18. Based on your class policy, explain how you will resolve a situation in which you observe a student looking at another student's paper during an examination. Whom will you notify first, the school administration or the student's parents? Please explain.

8.19. Based on your prior evaluation of grade-book software, download a demonstration software package and set up a hypothetical class of students. Base your evaluation on the grading system that you have created in question 8.5. For practice, enter some students' names and put in grades for the different tests and assignments. Is this software package user friendly? Why? Please explain.

8.20. Based on the concepts of validity and reliability, explain the possible effect of extra credit on course grades.

8.21. If a sixth-grade inclusion student reads at the second-grade level, should this student be penalized for not being able to read at grade level? Explain how differential grading could provide an option for reporting the progress of this inclusion student.

ANSWERS: CHECK FOR UNDERSTANDING

8.1. Letter grades, percentage, and pass/fail.
8.2. 72%
8.3. A percentage grading system is a much more precise way of reporting achievement.
8.4. through 8.11. The answers will vary for each of these; please see instructor.

ANSWERS: CHAPTER REVIEW QUESTIONS

8.12 through 8.19. The answers will vary for each of these; please see instructor.

8.20.   Giving away points poses a serious threat to the reliability and validity of test results. Therefore, it is our recommendation that you adhere to the recommendations for increased validity and reliability.

8.21.   The answers will vary; please see instructor.

INTERNET RESOURCES

www.csubak.edu/~jross/classes/GS390/Spreadsheets/ExcelBasics/ExcelBasics.HTML

This website provides spreadsheet basics for a user who is unfamiliar with spreadsheets. The site offers step-by-step instructions on how to create a spreadsheet.

http://office.microsoft.com/templates/default.aspx

Microsoft, which created Excel, includes templates on this site for creating spreadsheets. Some of the templates are designed for teacher grade books.

www.dy-regional.k12.ma.us/wixon/Course_Work/spreadsheet.htm

This site of Nathaniel H. Wixon Middle School, offers a comprehensive overview of spreadsheet applications for teachers.

http://storywind.net/education/mccarthy/lessons/exceltutorial.html

This website provides comprehensive information on the essentials of spreadsheet applications for teachers.

REFERENCES

Callahan, D. 2004. *The cheating culture*. New York: Harcourt.

FURTHER READING

Bradley, D. F., and M. B. Calvi. 1998. Grading modified assignments: Equity or compromise? *Teaching Exceptional Children* 31 and 2: 24–29.

Cureton, L. W. 1971. The history of grading practices. *Measurement in Education* 24: 1–8.

Guskey, T. R. 2001. Helping standards make the grade. *Educational Leadership* 591: 20–27.

Young, J. W. 1993. Grade adjustment methods. *Review of Educational Research* 63: 151–165.

Appendix

AREAS OF THE STANDARD NORMAL DISTRIBUTION

Z	.00	.01	.02	.03	.04	.05	.06	.07	.08	.09
0.0	.0000	.0040	.0080	.0120	.0160	.0199	.0239	.0279	.0319	.0359
0.1	.0398	.0438	.0478	.0517	.0557	.0596	.0636	.0675	.0714	.0753
0.2	.0793	.0832	.0871	.0910	.0948	.0987	.1026	.1064	.1103	.1141
0.3	.1179	.1217	.1255	.1293	.1331	.1368	.1406	.1443	.1480	.1517
0.4	.1554	.1591	.1628	.1664	.1700	.1736	.1772	.1808	.1844	.1879
0.5	.1915	.1950	.1985	.2019	.2054	.2088	.2123	.2157	.2190	.2224
0.6	.2257	.2291	.2324	.2357	.2389	.2422	.2454	.2486	.2517	.2549
0.7	.2580	.2611	.2642	.2673	.2704	.2734	.2764	.2794	.2823	.2852
0.8	.2881	.2910	.2939	.2967	.2995	.3023	.3051	.3078	.3106	.3133
0.9	.3159	.3186	.3212	.3238	.3264	.3289	.3315	.3340	.3365	.3389
1.0	.3413	.3438	.3461	.3485	.3508	.3531	.3554	.3577	.3599	.3621
1.1	.3643	.3665	.3686	.3708	.3729	.3749	.3770	.3790	.3810	.3830
1.2	.3849	.3869	.3888	.3907	.3925	.3944	.3962	.3980	.3997	.4015
1.3	.4032	.4049	.4066	.4082	.4099	.4115	.4131	.4147	.4162	.4177
1.4	.4192	.4207	.4222	.4236	.4251	.4265	.4279	.4292	.4306	.4319
1.5	.4332	.4345	.4357	.4370	.4382	.4394	.4406	.4418	.4429	.4441
1.6	.4452	.4463	.4474	.4484	.4495	.4505	.4515	.4525	.4535	.4545
1.7	.4554	.4564	.4573	.4582	.4591	.4599	.4608	.4616	.4625	.4633
1.8	.4641	.4649	.4656	.4664	.4671	.4678	.4686	.4693	.4699	.4706
1.9	.4713	.4719	.4726	.4732	.4738	.4744	.4750	.4756	.4761	.4767
2.0	.4772	.4778	.4783	.4788	.4793	.4798	.4803	.4808	.4812	.4817
2.1	.4821	.4826	.4830	.4834	.4838	.4842	.4846	.4850	.4854	.4857
2.2	.4861	.4864	.4868	.4871	.4875	.4878	.4881	.4884	.4887	.4890
2.3	.4893	.4896	.4898	.4901	.4904	.4906	.4909	.4911	.4913	.4916
2.4	.4918	.4920	.4922	.4925	.4927	.4929	.4931	.4932	.4934	.4936
2.5	.4938	.4940	.4941	.4943	.4945	.4946	.4948	.4949	.4951	.4952
2.6	.4953	.4955	.4956	.4957	.4959	.4960	.4961	.4962	.4963	.4964
2.7	.4965	.4966	.4967	.4968	.4969	.4970	.4971	.4972	.4973	.4974
2.8	.4974	.4975	.4976	.4977	.4977	.4978	.4979	.4979	.4980	.4981
2.9	.4981	.4982	.4982	.4983	.4984	.4984	.4985	.4985	.4986	.4986
3.0	.4987	.4987	.4987	.4988	.4988	.4989	.4989	.4989	.4990	.4990

Index

Note: Page numbers in *italics* refer to tables or figures.
Page numbers in **boldface** refer to equations or calculation examples.